ADVANCE PRAISE FOR *POWER PLAYS*:

Ted Case has added an important volume to the history of one of the most important public private partnerships ever conceived . . . the electrification of rural America. Through insightful research and novelist prose, he takes us on a journey of how rural electric cooperatives changed the course of history by engaging U.S. presidents over the past 75 years. Current leaders in the cooperative movement could use it as a playbook for the next 75 years.

—ADAM SCHWARTZ, Founder, The Cooperative Way

Nebraska Senator George Norris, who with House Speaker Sam Rayburn framed the Rural Electrification Act, observed that REA "will have made one of the greatest contributions toward the improvement of farm life that could possibly be imagined." In his astonishing book, author Ted Case tells how electric cooperatives took the battle to keep REA as the "greatest contribution" to a succession of abiding and antagonistic presidents.

—MARK GLAESS, Manager, Minnesota Rural Electric Association

"The forward march of America's not-for-profit, member-owned electric cooperatives has been closely intertwined with decisions made in the Oval Office. Ted Case brilliantly brings to life how relations with the nation's chief executive over the past seventy-five-plus years have impacted the ability of electric co-ops to fulfill their core mission: improving the rural quality of life."

—PERRY STAMBAUGH, Senior Director and Editor, *Rural Electric (RE) Magazine* and creator of the *Electric Cooperative Almanac*

The U.S. Presidency, Electric Cooperatives,
and the Transformation of Rural America

POWER
PLAYS

TED CASE

Rep. Aric Nesbitt,
Best wishes
Ted Case

Ordering Information

To order additional copies email: tedjcase@gmail.com.

Book design: Shannon Bodie, Lightbourne, Inc.
Index: Hassman Indexing Services
Cover source images: Corbis Images (light bulb),
                     iStockphoto (USA Presidential Seal)

ISBN: 978-0-9891829-0-4

10   9   8   7   6   5   4   3   2

CONTENTS

For Nicole,
who always does the right thing.

EXECUTIVE ORDER

ESTABLISHMENT OF THE RURAL ELECTRIFICATION ADMINISTRATION

By virtue of and pursuant to the authority vested in me under the Emergency Relief Appropriation Act of 1935, approved April 8, 1935 (Public Resolution No. 11, 74th Congress), I hereby establish an agency within the Government to be known as the "Rural Electrification Administration", the head thereof to be known as the Administrator.

I hereby prescribe the following duties and functions of the said Rural Electrification Administration to be exercised and performed by the Administrator thereof to be hereafter appointed:

To initiate, formulate, administer, and supervise a program of approved projects with respect to the generation, transmission, and distribution of electric energy in rural areas.

In the performance of such duties and functions, expenditures are hereby authorized for necessary supplies and equipment; law books and books of reference, directories, periodicals, newspapers and press clippings; travel expenses, including the expense of attendance at meetings when specifically authorized by the Administrator; rental at the seat of Government and elsewhere; purchase, operation and maintenance of passenger-carrying vehicles; printing and binding; and incidental expenses; and I hereby authorize the Administrator to accept and utilize such voluntary and uncompensated services and, with the consent of the State, such State and local officers and employees, and appoint, without regard to the provisions of the civil service laws, such officers and employees, as may be necessary, prescribe their duties and responsibilities and, without regard to the Classification Act of 1923, as amended, fix their compensation: **Provided**, That in so far as practicable, the persons employed under the authority of this Executive Order shall be selected from those receiving relief.

To the extent necessary to carry out the provisions of this Executive Order the Administrator is authorized to acquire, by purchase or by the power of eminent domain, any real property or any interest therein and improve, develop, grant, sell, lease (with or without the privilege of purchasing), or otherwise dispose of any such property or interest therein.

For the administrative expenses of the Rural Electrification Administration there is hereby allocated to the Administration from the appropriation made by the Emergency Relief Appropriation Act of 1935 the sum of $75,000. Allocations will be made hereafter for authorized projects.

Franklin D. Roosevelt

The White House,
May 11, 1935

7037

PREFACE

THE PRESIDENT OF THE UNITED STATES WAS GOING FISHING.
It was May 11, 1935, and Franklin Delano Roosevelt would soon
leave the White House for the Blue Ridge Mountains with Vice
President John Nance Garner and the Speaker of the U.S. House of
Representatives Joseph Byrns.[1] Normally, Roosevelt's Oval Office
was hosting up to fifteen meetings a day as FDR guided the nation
through the Great Depression.[2]

On this day, there were none. It was a clear day, the Oval Office
bathed in light from the giant windows filling the room's southern
curve. At 10:30 a.m., an "open-air" car was going to motor FDR
to the Woodmont Rod and Gun Club near the West Virginia and
Maryland border. After a day of trout fishing, there would be steaks,
political gossip, and a few cocktails. Before he could do any of this,
there was one piece of important presidential business.

FDR had to do something in 1935 about social security and
about creating jobs for the vast number of unemployed Americans.
But today, before he left, FDR planned to sign Executive Order 7037,
establishing "an agency within the Government to be known as the
Rural Electrification Administration . . ." The Executive Order had
been drafted by Morris Cooke, a talented engineer who had urged

---

The Executive Order establishing the Rural Electrification Administration.
President Franklin D. Roosevelt signed the Executive Order and then went fishing.

Roosevelt to read a "twelve-minute memo" that made the case for a national rural electrification plan.

The president knew something about the electric power industry. As governor of New York, Roosevelt had consulted experts, seeking to develop hydropower on the St. Lawrence River. It was Cooke, however, who had set up this new rural electrification agency after FDR failed to commit to a specific plan or offer Cooke a sense of direction.[3]

FDR was feeling the pressure to act. Both the American Farm Bureau Federation and the National Grange had passed resolutions urging federal action to provide light and power to the countryside. A month before, Congress had allocated $100 million for construction of rural distribution lines as part of a relief project. All FDR had to do was authorize the plan that would allow $75,000 for putting the administrative, technical, and operational jigsaw together.[4]

Only 10 percent of the farms across America had electricity and those without it were living a life of drudgery.[5] FDR had witnessed the difficulties in Georgia near his cottage at Warm Springs. He had seen hardship up close with U.S. Senator George Norris of Nebraska as they toured the Tennessee Valley after FDR's election in 1932.[6] There, only two of every one hundred farms had electricity. Sanitation was primitive, medical care was sparse, and infant mortality rates were astonishingly high. In the first one hundred days of his presidency, FDR together with Norris led the passage of the Tennessee Valley Authority Act, creating a series of dams that would transform the region through inexpensive power, flood control, and improved navigation.

FDR was aware of an experimental TVA cooperative in Corinth, Mississippi, which showed promise bringing electricity to farmers.[7] Perhaps this concept could be expanded across the nation.

Roosevelt picked up his pen. It was going to be a massive job, and he was pleased that he had convinced Cooke to become the first administrator of this new REA, located in the basement of the Interior Department.[8] FDR signed his name across the bottom right corner of the document. The blueprint was in place. FDR's job for the day was done.

All they had to do now was electrify five million farms.

INTRODUCTION

*"A friendly executive in the White House is essential to the growth of
the program. A hostile president could cripple the program
or use his power to cause it to wither or die."[1]*

FORMER NRECA GENERAL MANAGER ROBERT D. PARTRIDGE

O N FEBRUARY 10, 2011, PRESIDENT BARACK OBAMA WAS
speaking in enemy territory, at least in his capacity as the
nation's highest-ranking Chicago Bears fan. "How many of you
are Green Bay fans?" he asked students at Northern Michigan
University in Marquette. Cheers from the raucous crowd confirmed
what the president already knew. "I've been seeing too many Green
Bay fans," he quipped.[2] He wasn't there, however, to talk about
football. This tech-savvy college crowd had been selected to showcase a White House initiative to connect every corner of America to
the digital age through expanded wireless broadband access.

At a podium under a backdrop that read *Winning the Future*,
Obama promoted the benefits of universal broadband. "It's about a
rural community in Iowa or Alabama where farmers can monitor
weather across the state and markets across the globe." Conceding
that it would not be easy to connect the nation's most remote areas,

he noted there was precedent. "We do big things," Obama said.
"That's who we are."

Big things. Undoubtedly, the president's speechwriters had sat
around a cramped office in the West Wing, brainstorming examples
that demonstrated America's can-do spirit. They came up with three:
the transcontinental railroad, Interstate Highway System, and one
that seemed to have particular relevance on this day—the Rural
Electrification Administration (REA).

When Barack Obama was born in 1961, nearly 97 percent of
the country was electrified.[3] He had no personal knowledge of
kerosene lanterns and washboards, but he told the crowd how rural
Americans seventy-five years before could not even watch a movie
in a local theater unless it was equipped with a diesel engine. He also
spoke of the president who deserved much of the credit for changing the way rural Americans lived.

"FDR set up the Rural Electrification Administration to help
bring power to vast swaths of America that were still in darkness,"
Obama said. "Companies said that building lines to rural areas
would be too costly."

It was a powerful message, delivered by a gifted messenger.
N. Duane Noland, CEO of the Association of Illinois Electric
Cooperatives, served in the Illinois legislature and recalls a junior
colleague speaking for the first time in the state Senate chamber. "I
scanned the room when I heard that baritone voice and his command of the microphone," Noland said.[4] The speaker was then state
senator Barack Obama.

Now, before the college students, the president modulated his
voice, jabbing his right hand in the air for emphasis. "Once power
lines were laid down," Obama declared, "electricity flowed to farms
across the country, transforming millions of lives."[5] Of course, it
wasn't that easy, but President Obama was not giving a tutorial on

electrical engineering. He was talking about presidential leadership. And there are few better examples of presidential leadership than what FDR did for rural electrification.

"FDR knew so much about so many things," said Pulitzer Prize-winning author David M. Kennedy, "but what he knew the greatest about was public power."[6]

The power lines that Obama spoke of did not go up overnight. The for-profit power companies showed little interest in taking advantage of the REA lending program. Neither did the municipal utilities. This left cooperatives as the last option to bring electricity to farms. Co-ops had marketing experience, but REA administrator Morris Cooke wondered if the average farmer would require more assistance than the REA could provide.[7] It also became clear that the REA Executive Order was insufficient. The REA needed steady funding that only could come from Capitol Hill.

In 1936, U.S. Senator George Norris and U.S. Representative Sam Rayburn of Texas beat back the for-profit power companies to make the REA the law of the land.[8] Even with Rayburn's legendary political skills, the REA Act passed a key congressional committee by only one vote. Today, it is hard to comprehend how close this landmark law was to defeat, potentially setting back the rural electrification movement for years.

President Obama, in his speech, detailed the consequences of this narrow victory. "There's a well-known story of a Texas family returning home the first night their farmhouse was hooked up, and a woman thought it was on fire."[9] The president paused for dramatic effect. "And her daughter said, 'No, Mama, the lights are on.'" The college students listened with rapt attention. "Think about that," Obama said. "That wasn't that long ago."

It was 1939. The family the president spoke of lived in the Texas Hill Country served by Pedernales Electric Cooperative. It was a story made possible by a young Texas congressman—and future president—named Lyndon Baines Johnson (LBJ).

Time will tell if deploying broadband to rural areas is the next great American success story. But President Obama was right about one thing: The story of rural electrification is synonymous with how presidential leadership can help the country achieve big things. It is the story of men such as FDR and LBJ, and their partnership with utilities that Morris Cooke selected almost by default: America's electric co-ops.

In 2013, more than nine hundred electric co-ops serve forty-two million consumers in forty-seven states. As independent, locally owned businesses, each electric co-op is different. But they share a common thread: Co-ops are owned by the consumers they serve and these consumers share responsibility for the co-op's success or failure.

In the early days, electric co-ops were struggling. Many could not get materials or insurance at reasonable rates. They needed a national voice. At the urging of interested members of Congress and REA officials, electric co-ops formed the National Rural Electric Cooperative Association (NRECA) in 1942. NRECA started with only $23,000 in the bank and a small staff.[10] Over the next several decades, it emerged into a major force on the American political scene, carrying the electric co-op message to the White House and Congress. It is also an organization that takes its heritage seriously.

The eleventh floor of the headquarters in Arlington, Virginia, serves as a shrine to electric co-op legends. Photographs of Harry Truman and John F. Kennedy line the walls of the library. For employees, learning the iconic stories about electric co-ops and the presidency is almost a rite of passage: FDR speaking to forty thousand people at a co-op dedication in Georgia; Richard Nixon attempting to eliminate the REA lending program by press release on New Year's Eve weekend in 1972; and Bill Clinton's shocking revelation about the REA in his 1993 State of the Union address.

These are part of a rich and fascinating electric co-op history. But it is an incomplete, one-sided history. From experience, I knew what electric co-op leaders thought of our presidents. But what did our presidents think of electric co-ops? What was their background with rural electrification? And what was the political and historical context that influenced their decision-making on electric co-op issues?

Through interviews, oral histories, and stacks of presidential memos and documents, I attempt to recreate this history and tell the electric co-op story in a different way than ever before. Not only from the perspective of electric co-op leaders, but from the president himself.

This book does not purport to be the history of electric co-ops or the various federal programs that helped electrify America. Rather, it is a series of defining moments in the history of electric co-ops and the presidency. These snapshots in time often occur, not surprisingly, inside the White House. But they also occur in the unlikeliest of places: a packed stadium in Georgia, the rear car of a luxury train, and a barren field in Pennsylvania.

While the REA provides a flashpoint for epic legislative battles, electric co-op history also collides with some of the most important events of the past seventy-five years: FDR's "purge" of dissident Democrats, the classic 1948 Truman-Dewey presidential campaign, JFK's Cuban Missile Crisis, the Vietnam War, Nixon's Watergate scandal, and the tragic events of September 11, 2001. Taken together, these episodes vividly demonstrate that electric co-ops occupy a place in history far beyond stringing wire down a lonely country road.

There are countless electric co-op leaders who helped build NRECA into one of the most significant trade associations in

Washington, D.C. But until early 2013, there were only four men who led the organization during the last seventy years. I trace the careers of these four political leaders—men who are not household names but who dominated the electric co-op world as general managers and CEOs of NRECA. "We were different men for our time," said former NRECA CEO Glenn English. "But I'd like to think we were the right men for our time."[11]

- **Clyde Ellis**: A driven, impatient former congressman from Arkansas who led the association for twenty-six years. Described as equal parts taskmaster and motivator, Ellis almost single-handedly shaped NRECA's early development, relentlessly advocating for the REA and federal water resource programs.[12] He built strong friendships with four different presidents, but went head-to-head with Dwight D. Eisenhower in one of the most high-profile legislative battles in electric co-op history.

- **Bob Partridge**: Possessing a rare blend of technical expertise and interpersonal skills, Partridge became general manager in 1968 after rising through the ranks of REA and NRECA. A Missourian and a recipient of the Bronze Star for valor in World War II, Partridge was forced into a different kind of battle on Friday, December 29, 1972, when President Nixon attempted to eliminate the REA. Considered one of the darkest hours in electric co-op history, Partridge's steady hand in the aftermath of "Black Friday" solidified NRECA's standing as a grass-roots power.

- **Bob Bergland**: An affable, populist former Minnesota congressman from humble roots, Bergland also served as

U.S. Secretary of Agriculture under President Jimmy Carter. He became NRECA's general manager in 1984 during the tumultuous Reagan years, culminating his storied career by reforming the REA with President Bill Clinton.

- **Glenn English**: A ten-term Oklahoma U.S. Representative with prodigious skills honed from a lifetime in the political arena, English took the helm as CEO in 1994. Facing a more complex electric utility industry than his predecessors, English navigated electric co-ops through the classic "PMA sale fight of 1995," electric utility deregulation, landmark national energy legislation, and a perilous debate over climate change. He retired in early 2013 after nineteen years of service to NRECA.

While I examine the federal infrastructure that helped electrify the nation—the REA, the TVA, and the federal Power Marketing Administrations (PMAs)—ultimately this book is more a story of politics than it is of power lines. It is more about elections than electrons. It is about how electric co-ops accumulated political strength, exercised it, and fought to retain it. And it is about how presidents either aligned with electric co-ops or challenged their political strength to meet their own agenda. The story spans more than seventy-five years, evolving from a time when darkness pervaded rural America, to a more recent time when political leaders such as President Obama only knew these stories from a book.

This story begins when the lights were still coming on in rural America.

In the spring of 1938, President Franklin Delano Roosevelt sat
in the Oval Office studying a map of Georgia.[13] The small town of
Barnesville had been marked, where a rural electrification project
was near completion, and would soon have a public dedication.
REA dedications were now occurring all over the country, typically
with a planting of a pole, a mock burial of a kerosene lamp, and
long-winded political speeches.[14] FDR had never personally dedicated an electric co-op, and he looked at the event in Barnesville as
an opportunity—in more ways than one.

The REA was on the move. Requests to establish electric co-ops
were flooding the agency. Rural leaders, primarily farmers and
ranchers, had accepted the daunting challenge to run their own utility, aided by REA lawyers, management experts, and engineers.

The REA was on the move in Plains, Georgia, where James Earl
Carter, Sr., became an electric co-op leader, teaching his young son,
Jimmy, about political involvement.[15] It was on the move in Texas
as U.S. Representative Lyndon Johnson lobbied the president in
his attempt to electrify the Hill Country. And it was on the move
because of men like U.S. Senator Harry Truman of Missouri, who
supported REA funding, even though the president's secretary—
much less Roosevelt himself—rarely returned Truman's calls.[16]

President Roosevelt was now in a political valley. Only two
years before, he had defeated Alf Landon of Kansas in the 1936
presidential election by a landslide. The country had rewarded
his New Deal accomplishments, but a recession and his ill-fated
scheme to pack the U.S. Supreme Court with friendly justices had
started a Democratic revolt in Congress. That is why in the Oval
Office that day, FDR hosted a shy U.S. attorney from Georgia
named Lawrence Camp.[17]

FDR wanted men like Camp elected to the U.S. Senate to
help kick-start his legislative agenda. Roosevelt also needed the

right forum to unveil an audacious plan to reverse his political fortune. John Carmody, the fiery REA administrator, also visited the Oval Office that day and observed the Georgia map on the easel. Carmody must have known this would be no ordinary REA dedication.

And it wasn't. That August, when the project was complete, FDR would travel to Barnesville for the most famous electric co-op dedication in history, though not for the reason most people believe. President Roosevelt planned to bring rural Georgians out of the darkness and begin a battle for the soul of the Democratic Party.

His presidency would never again be the same.

1

THE BATTLE
OF BARNESVILLE

I T WAS AUGUST 11, 1938, THE DATE THE OLD FARMER'S ALMANAC
called the end of the "dog days of summer." The crowd massing
at the Gordon Military College stadium in Barnesville had traveled
there on foot, horseback, carriage, wagon, automobile, pickup truck,
and tractor.[1] President Franklin Delano Roosevelt had arrived by
private train from Warm Springs, some sixty miles away. While the
crowd withered in the heat, Roosevelt was shaded with other digni-
taries under the flag-decked wooden platform, appearing cool and
confident in his fine summer suit.[2]

The smell of pine and peaches was in the air, and FDR's spirits
were high.[3] He was rejuvenated, not only from a boat cruise along the
equator where he'd landed a 230-pound shark, but because he was
beloved here in Georgia, having captured an incredible 87 percent
of the vote in the 1936 election. Today, in front of forty thousand
people, FDR planned to test how far he could take that affection.

Franklin D. Roosevelt speaks to forty thousand people in Barnesville, Georgia. After
dedicating the new co-op, he called for the defeat of U.S. Senator Walter George,
a senior member of President Roosevelt's own party.

He was in Barnesville for two reasons. The first was to celebrate one of the stunning achievements of the New Deal: the three-year-old REA. Already, the agency had helped construct seventy-three thousand miles of electric lines, reaching more than three hundred thousand farms and ranches. On this day, 357 more families in Georgia would be brought out of darkness by a partnership between the REA and a newly formed electric co-op, the Lamar Electric Membership Corporation.[4]

FDR's other reason for being there was hatched in the Oval Office earlier in the year. It was why Barnesville, normally a quiet hamlet of four thousand residents, had, for at least one day, become the center of America's political universe. FDR was going to do no less than begin his campaign to transform the Democratic Party.

In a maneuver considered a breathtaking departure from American political tradition, FDR planned to call for the defeat of incumbent U.S. Senator Walter George, a conservative Democrat and a senior member of Roosevelt's *own* political party.[5] To make his point exceedingly clear, Roosevelt was going to repudiate George as they appeared together on the same platform, only a few feet away.

Walter George had it coming, at least according to FDR. He had earned the president's wrath by joining with conservative Democrats to oppose FDR's court-packing fiasco. FDR was not tolerant of dissident Democrats; for him, the big tent of the Democratic Party was only so big. So he was going to "purge" them from the party and replace them with liberals who shared his philosophy. By intervening in state primaries, Roosevelt risked alienating hundreds of thousands of their supporters.

The day before, Roosevelt had casually endorsed George's primary opponent, Lawrence Camp, who was also sitting on the platform. Roosevelt, however, had not yet laid down a frontal attack on George. Many of FDR's advisers, including political confidante

Jim Farley, thought the plan was political suicide. "Boss, I think you're foolish," Farley told Roosevelt. "I don't think George can be beaten."[6] It was too late now. The dedication in Barnesville was under way, with the state's political elite fawning over FDR.

Georgia's junior senator, Richard Russell, led off the festivities, proclaiming that Roosevelt was "the greatest exponent of liberal democracy and equality of opportunity of his generation."[7] Georgia Governor Ed Rivers introduced the president with such lavish praise that someone in the crowd finally shouted, "Turn him off!"[8]

By the time it was FDR's turn to speak, some in the crowd had fainted from dehydration. Blisters from the harsh sun were forming on the necks of others. But no one was going anywhere. For the last twenty-three years of his life, Roosevelt could not stand unassisted, but once he got to the podium, he took command.

Like all modern presidents, Roosevelt had a team of speech-writers, but the final draft was always his work.[9] Looming over the draped banners with the insignias of the radio networks covering the event, FDR told the crowd he had first come to Warm Springs "fourteen years ago" as a "Democratic Yankee." There was, however, one discordant note at his first stay at Warm Springs. He said his electricity bill informed him "the charge was eighteen cents per kilowatt hour—about four times as much as I was paying in . . . Hyde Park."[10] Someone yelled, "They were just trying to rob us poor people!"[11] Even with the interruptions, FDR was unflappable.

"That light bill started my long study of proper utility charges for electric current, started in my mind, the whole subject of getting electricity into farm homes throughout the United States. So my friends it can be said . . . that a little cottage at Warm Springs, Georgia, was the birthplace of the Rural Electrification Administration . . ."[12] FDR could barely finish a sentence over the shouting.

"Electricity is a modern necessity of life, not a luxury," he told them. "That necessity ought to be found in every village, in every house, and on every farm in every part of the United States. The dedication of this [REA] project in Georgia today is a symbol of the progress we are making—and we are not going to stop!"[13] The stadium erupted in applause. Most accounts of FDR's speech overlook what followed, and its consequences for American political history.[14] There was more than celebrating the REA. There was also the messy swamp of Georgia politics, a subject into which FDR was wading neck deep.

Senator George was now paying attention.[15] As a supporter of the Georgia Power Company, which fought the establishment of electric co-ops, he'd seemed uninterested when FDR exalted the REA. But he appeared to listen closely as FDR changed the subject to the upcoming Democratic primary and said he felt "no hesitation in telling you what I would do if I could vote here next month."[16]

Appearing to weigh each word and phrase for maximum affect, Roosevelt said George could not "be classified as belonging to the liberal school of thought." Roosevelt called George his good friend and then eviscerated him. He accused George of paying "lip service" to his objectives, and that he and other dissidents "had not raised their little fingers actively to attain the objectives themselves."[17] George shifted in his chair, his gray hair blowing in the slight breeze. *The New York Times* noted that, "observers who had traveled with the president for years said they could not recall when he attacked like he did today."[18]

The liberal in this election, FDR said, was Camp, "a man who honestly believes that many things must be done and done now to improve the economic and social conditions of the country." By now, the crowd was awestruck as Roosevelt told them if he were able

In 1935, only 10 percent of the farms had electricity, and those without it
were living a life of drudgery. Rural farmwives spent twenty days more
per year washing clothes than their urban counterparts.

to vote in the September primaries, "I would most assuredly cast my
ballot for Lawrence Camp."

Scattered applause followed, mixed with boos and catcalls from
George's loyal followers. His mission accomplished, Roosevelt
pivoted back to safer ground. "In dedicating this important project
today," Roosevelt proclaimed, "I want to express once more my abiding faith that as a nation we are moving steadily and surely toward a
better way of living for all of our people . . . It is only one symbol; it
is one hill out of ten thousand which must be captured."

The president basked in the adulation, before a hush swept
through the stadium. Forty thousand people held their breath as
Senator Walter George rose from his chair.

FDR may have had political motives that day, but the REA dedication was no sideshow. Shimmering in the sun on the stadium field was a display that would soon improve rural lives more than they could imagine, including refrigerators, ranges, washing machines, and radios.[19] These appliances would help curb diseases commonplace because of spoilage, such as dysentery. They would help improve diets dangerously lacking in essential vitamins, iron, and protein. The electric washers would end the ceaseless toil of washing clothes, which for farmwives amounted to twenty days more per year than their urban counterparts.

Paul Wood, CEO of the Georgia Electric Membership Corporation, which represents the state's electric co-ops, said, "I wonder often if FDR had not come to Warm Springs to seek relief from polio, and not experienced firsthand what poverty existed in rural areas, how long it would have been before rural areas had electricity."[20] The families at the Lamar co-op would not have to wait much longer. First, however, they needed to watch Senator George confront the president of the United States.

———— • ◆ • ————

Walter George approached the podium and took control of the microphone. "Mr. President, I regret that you have taken the occasion to question my democracy and to attack my record," George said, his voice cool and steady. "I want you to know that I accept the challenge—in the friendly spirit in which it was given."[21] George's composure seemed to unnerve FDR. The president leaned back into the microphone.

"God bless you, Walter," Roosevelt said. "Let's always be friends."[22]

The crowd cheered, though it was unclear for whom they were cheering.[23] They could all agree on one thing: Friendship between the two men was out of the question. Roosevelt had unleashed a bitter, personal attack on a member of his own party, and there was no turning back now. The purge of 1938 had officially begun in Georgia.

But somebody needed to turn on the lights. Accounts vary, but some believe that REA administrator Carmody flipped the power switch when Roosevelt, disconcerted by the confrontation with George, hastily left the platform. It is also plausible that the Secret Service would not allow FDR anywhere near electrical current.

By day's end, no one seemed to care who turned on the lights once electricity started flowing to Georgia families along 144 miles of rural power lines.[24] Grover Worsham was eight years old when his father took him to the speech.[25] Perhaps he did not fully understand what electric co-op membership meant for him, but Worsham quickly learned the benefits.

"Our house was wired, but there was no electricity," he recounted. "When we came back there was electricity. It was real unusual. I remember it all."

Thomas Weldon attended, too, watching from his father's shoulders.[26] He was only a boy, but years later he would take over as manager of the electric co-op and lead it for a quarter-century.

The homes and farms surrounding Barnesville, like towns all over rural America, would be transformed. By the end of 1938, 22 percent of the country was electrified.

After Roosevelt left the state, George wasted no time telling voters that FDR's intervention was "a second march through Georgia." Roosevelt also marched on South Carolina, Maryland, and Iowa, lending his power and prestige to oust other conservative Democratic legislators. The question remained: Could Roosevelt by force of personality defeat popular incumbents and begin his quest for party realignment?

On September 14, Georgia voters went to the polls and delivered the president their answer. In a stinging rebuke, George drubbed Lawrence Camp in the primary. Camp finished a distant third and even lost his home county. A political disaster was in the making, the only election in which it can be said FDR was crushed. The four main targets of Roosevelt's purge easily turned away his attacks, sailing to renomination and re-election.[27] In addition to empowering conservative Democrats, a weakened FDR put New Deal candidates in jeopardy. Republicans exploited this weakness and picked up eighty-one seats in the House and eight in the Senate.[28]

The lights came on that year in parts of rural America, but the New Deal coalition dimmed. More significantly, the Republican establishment was emboldened, believing they could finally remove FDR from the White House in 1940. "Clearly, President Roosevelt could not run for a third term even if he so desired," wrote Washington newsman Raymond Clapper.[29]

There was a bright spot for the Democrats as a young Arkansan named Clyde Ellis won a congressional seat, running on a platform of rural electrification and river development. Few men over the next quarter-century would have more impact on electric co-ops than Ellis, but he was entering a different Democratic Party than FDR had led for the past six years. In fact, it hardly seemed Roosevelt's party at all.

Susan Dunn, author of the book *Roosevelt's Purge: How FDR Fought to Change the Democratic Party*, believed what happened in Barnesville "represented more than a scheme to restart the New Deal. It was a precursor of a historic transformation of American political parties."[30]

Conservative southern Democrats emerged as a potent force that would dominate the American political landscape for decades. Over time, the Democratic Party could no longer hold conservative

Democrats in their big tent, and the once solid Democratic South would be solid no more.

Roosevelt's presidency would soon shift from the New Deal to World War II. The name of the co-op in Barnesville would later change to Southern Rivers Electric Membership Corporation. The area would transform from the "Buggy Capital of the South" to a bedroom community of Atlanta. Some things, however, remained constant. Raleigh Henry, the fourth general manager of Southern Rivers, said FDR's historic speech in Barnesville "is still a topic of conversation seventy-five years later."[31]

FDR learned a bitter lesson in a most public way and never again challenged another Democrat. When Harry Truman asked for help in 1940, Roosevelt aide Steve Early replied it was FDR's "invariable practice not to take part in primary contests."[32] For electric co-op leaders, FDR's presence in Barnesville was truly historic. The champion of the REA never dedicated another electric co-op.

———————— • ◆ • ————————

World War II helped President Roosevelt regain his political footing, and he was re-elected in 1940 and 1944. There were now over three hundred electric co-ops across the country, selling more electricity than the engineers ever imagined. State co-op associations were forming and beginning to flex political muscle. The co-ops had also organized nationally with a leader, Clyde Ellis, well known to FDR.

After losing a U.S. Senate campaign in 1942, Ellis took charge of the National Rural Electric Cooperative Association. FDR had even committed to a persistent Ellis that he'd speak at NRECA's annual meeting as soon as the war ended.

In March 1945, the war appeared to be at end. Roosevelt's decision to reach down the army chain of command to tap Dwight D.

Eisenhower as supreme commander had led to a sweeping victory in Europe. It was aided by a U.S. war machine powered by two agencies created during FDR's presidency that were also important energy suppliers to electric co-ops: the giant dams in the Pacific Northwest under the authority of the Bonneville Power Administration (BPA), and hydroelectric projects operated by the TVA.

On March 29, 1945, FDR was frail and weary, no longer the robust leader who commanded the stage in Barnesville.[33] FDR ignored the White House doctors who requested he slow down. Too much was happening in the world that needed his attention: The Americans had raised a flag at Iwo Jima in the South Pacific, U.S. and Allied troops had invaded Okinawa, and the American Third Army was marching through Germany.[34] There were endless meetings and mountains of paperwork. At 10:30 a.m., he was wheeled downstairs for another day of work.[35]

FDR had a full slate of meetings on March 29, including with his secretary of state, the British ambassador, and two U.S. Senators. His staff was worried. Sitting at his desk, Roosevelt looked pale. "It was more than his health," wrote historian Jim Bishop. "White House intimates had the impression that his spirit, his will, had been crushed."[36]

"Did you get any rest at Hyde Park, Mr. President?" asked his secretary, Grace Tully.

"Yes, child, but not nearly enough," replied Roosevelt. "I shall be glad to get down South."[37]

He was traveling to Warm Springs later in the day, where his policies had dramatically improved the lives of the residents in the region. TVA had helped modernize the South by developing the economic potential of one of the nation's great river basins. And in the ten years of its existence, the REA had emancipated over two million people living on farms from lives of drudgery and darkness.[38]

If, as Roosevelt told the crowd in Barnesville, the little cottage in Warm Springs had been the birthplace of the REA, its formative years had taken place in the Oval Office. It was in the Oval Office in 1939 that Ellis, then a first-term Arkansas congressman, lobbied FDR to reconsider his controversial decision to move the REA to the U.S. Department of Agriculture.[39] FDR countered that with a war looming he needed fewer people walking through the Oval Office door.

"As long as I am president," Roosevelt told Ellis, "you'll have no need to worry."[40] After the REA was transferred, administrator John Carmody resigned in protest.[41] For Roosevelt, getting the right person to replace Carmody was essential. FDR told his staff "it was difficult to find the right man for administrator because the man had to be a builder and at the same time a finance man."[42] FDR believed he knew the right man. In a move that could have dramatically changed the twentieth-century American political landscape, Roosevelt had brought thirty-year-old Lyndon Baines Johnson into the Oval Office and offered him the REA job. Johnson was flattered and pondered the offer, but ultimately rejected it. He was afraid, he said, of being "sidetracked." His ambition, it seemed, was limitless.

Around noon in the Oval Office on that late March day, Grace Tully watched FDR sign a prayer book for his grandson, believing it would be his last White House signature for some time.[43] She noticed the absence of his "long optimistic monologues." Another visitor could not bear to watch the way the president's hand shook, even when reposed on his lap.

The meetings continued. Roosevelt had a courtesy call at 12:30 p.m., with Lucius Clay, who had been named to replace James Byrnes as head of the U.S. military government in Germany. Byrnes was also present for the discussion. There was nothing to indicate this brief meeting would be significant or based on FDR's health, even prudent.

Byrnes was still prepared.[44] He knew how FDR could control the agenda of a meeting, sitting back with his long-stemmed cigarette holder and throwing his visitors off-guard. Be ready for anything, Byrnes advised. "He's going to ask you some trick question like, 'What would you do if in Heidelberg during the night Germans rose up and attacked and killed a few soldiers.'"

FDR greeted the men and reminisced about his childhood in Germany. The country was now in ruins from Allied bombardments. Distributing food and rebuilding the transportation system would be Clay's top priorities. The president, however, had another priority. The real problem in postwar Europe, Roosevelt told Clay, would be "energy."

Central Europe could be rebuilt, FDR proclaimed, with a "TVA-like program for the entire continent." The men were taken aback. FDR believed this idea would have "great meaning and great significance" for all of Europe, just as it had for the southern United States. The unprecedented rate of economic growth and development that occurred in TVA's first decade led FDR to believe this success could be transferred to a war-torn region. Part of this success had been the unpretentious beginning of TVA co-ops in the rear of a furniture store in Corinth, Mississippi.

TVA officials had met with local leaders and agreed to form a cooperative.[45] In 1934, the result was the Alcorn Electric Power Association. Then the scrutiny began. Did farmers have the sophistication and business savvy to govern their co-op, keep the electricity flowing, and pay the bills? The question was answered a year later when Alcorn expanded its service territory, cut rates by 50 percent, and paid taxes. Michael Callahan, CEO of the Electric Power Associations of Mississippi, said, "Alcorn was an experiment whose success proved the feasibility of a cooperative to get electricity to rural populations of Mississippi."[46] Soon, the experiment expanded across the United States.

Now, FDR wanted to bring the experiment to Europe. He was clearly enjoying his Oval Office meeting with Byrnes and Clay, but Roosevelt aide Steve Early thought it had gone long enough.[47] Considered the first modern press secretary, Early had persuaded the media to hide the extent of the president's debilitation, but he could not convince FDR to end this meeting. According to Clay, FDR waved him off two or three times.

Finally, Roosevelt relented and the meeting broke up. Lucius Clay had passed muster without being asked a single question. Later, Clay was asked why he did not talk at the meeting. "Because I was so shocked watching him that I don't think I could have made a sensible reply," Clay said. "We've been talking to a dying man."

At 4 p.m. that day, the presidential motorcade whisked FDR to Union Station for the train trip to Warm Springs.[48] He asked his staff to make sure the conductor did not "set any speed records." Roosevelt's bony frame simply could not handle the force of the curves. The train rolled through the wooded Virginia battlefields, part of an America where 50 percent of the farms now had electricity. Much work needed to be done, but Roosevelt had set the stage for the REA to finish the job. It would only be a matter of time before all Americans had electricity.

He would not live to see it.

President Roosevelt never returned to Washington, D.C., passing away in Warm Springs on April 12, 1945, of a cerebral hemorrhage. Perhaps it was fitting that during his final day in the White House, FDR was reflecting on one of his signature achievements.

At the seventy-fifth anniversary of the REA in 2010, then-NRECA CEO Glenn English went to the Little White House in Warm Springs. "I believe President Roosevelt would be pleased to see the results of his grand creation," English said.[49] Historian Jean

Edward Smith wrote, "With the possible exception of the Federal Deposit Insurance Corporation, no single action by the New Deal had a greater impact on daily life in the American countryside than rural electrification."[50]

Bringing the benefits of rural electrification to the rest of the world soon became a hallmark for presidents who succeeded him. TVA also captured the imagination of other countries, and scores of projects around the globe bear the imprint of unified development of resources.

Fate had also given Lucius Clay a place in history. His one and only meeting with President Roosevelt to discuss postwar Germany had turned into a historic discussion of the benefits of water resource development. In an ordinary Oval Office meeting that turned extraordinary, there was an additional distinction.

It was also Roosevelt's last official appointment in the White House.[51]

———— ◆ ————

On April 12, 1945, Steve Early phoned Vice President Harry Truman as he sat in a hideaway office in the U.S. Capitol enjoying a cocktail with Speaker Sam Rayburn.[52] Early's voice sounded tense. Truman was instructed to come as "quickly and as quietly" as he could to the White House. He was not told the president was dead, but he went out the door alone. Then he started to run. Blunt-spoken, plain-living, and proud of his Missouri roots, Truman was now the most unlikely man to be an American president.[53]

While he had earned FDR's gratitude, there was one thing FDR had not told him.[54] The massive dams on the Columbia River powered a mysterious electrical load devouring more electricity than the electric co-ops and municipal utilities in the Northwest used combined.[55] It was the energy needed to produce plutonium for the world's first atomic bombs. Truman's decision to use these atomic bombs to destroy the Japanese cities of Hiroshima and Nagasaki helped end the war with Japan.

America transitioned from war to peace, and rural electrification was in high gear. In 1944, Congress had passed the Pace Act (named after its author, U.S. Representative Stephen Pace of Georgia) in an effort to accelerate line construction.[56] The legislation extended REA's mission beyond its 1946 expiration date and fixed REA interest rates at 2 percent. Soon, more than forty thousand consumers a month were being connected to electric co-op lines.[57] The REA had also hired Bob Partridge, who was looking for work after returning from World War II. He stayed there for fifteen years. "I had never worked with people with such missionary zeal, and it was contagious," Partridge said.[58]

However, by late 1946, not enough people had found work and the economy was faltering. Republicans seized control of the U.S. Congress that fall and wanted the Holy Grail of the White House. By 1948, President Harry Truman, with his party split three ways, found himself an underdog in the election against New York Governor Thomas E. Dewey.

Truman had been all but written off, but he believed he was on the right side of the issues. In the fall of 1948, he was going to climb aboard a luxury train and remind voters, among other things, who had electrified rural America. The night before he started his now famous Whistle-stop campaign, Truman made a surprise visit to electric co-op leaders. He did not seem intimidated by the task ahead; the message he brought was striking in its certitude. Unlike every political pundit and pollster in the nation, Harry Truman was sure about what the headlines would read the day after the election.

Truman defeats Dewey.

Clyde Ellis said his good friend Harry Truman would be
remembered "as one of our greatest presidents."

2

HOW ABOUT
THAT FARM VOTE?

O N September 16, 1948,[1] on the eve of a grueling
campaign trip that would take him twenty-one thousand
miles across America,[2] President Harry S. Truman made an unan-
nounced visit to a NRECA regional meeting held in Washington,
D.C.[3] His plans were not initially made public, and the event does
not even show up on his official schedule. Yet he appeared at the
Washington Hotel before two hundred fifty electric co-op leaders
because, unlike many in a politically fickle town, they had not
abandoned him. It did not matter that his GOP opponent, Governor
Thomas Dewey, held a commanding thirteen-point lead in the
polls.[4] It did not matter that almost everyone, including the president's own mother-in-law, believed Truman was certain to lose.
Electric co-op leaders were standing by Harry Truman.[5]

But it was more than politics that brought him there, though
NRECA's Clyde Ellis lobbied the White House staff for Truman to
appear, almost to the point of harassment. The sixty-four-year-old
Truman had a connection with the group, forged from growing up
on a farm with no electricity, water, or plumbing, from cooking on

a coal stove and knowing the hand pump would freeze solid in the winter.

His talk at 8:30 that evening was impromptu and nostalgic of his days as a loyal U.S. Senate supporter of electric co-ops.[6] "I remember the terrific fight which was made to prevent the passage of the rural electrification law," Truman told electric co-op leaders. "This organization and rural electrification have brought things to the farmers that they never dreamed of when I was a kid on the farm."

He spoke of Missouri and his farm where his nephew, also named Harry Truman, now lived, making use of the modern conveniences available because of electricity. Truman missed the old farm in Missouri, but he was not ready for Tom Dewey to send him back there. Political pundits were already chattering about who would serve in the Dewey administration. Rumors circulated that C.A. Sorensen, president of the Nebraska Association of Public Power Districts, was on the short list for REA administrator.[7] (Sorensen's son Ted would soon become a trusted adviser to Senator John F. Kennedy and play a central part in his relationship with electric co-ops.)

Truman was undaunted by both his electoral challenge and the obstacles of serving the farmer at the end of the line. "I hope you continue to actively fight for *expansion* until every farm in America has the necessary power," he said. "As long as I am president . . . I, myself, shall continue that fight."[8]

The expansion that Truman spoke of was continuing at a blistering rate. Two houses were being connected each minute of every working day, not only in the isolated reaches of the Dakotas and Montana but in denser areas of the East where some had missed electricity the first time around.[9] Truman's speech was a test run for one of the defining issues of his campaign: rural electrification. "I am going to try telling the country just exactly what the issues are,"

Truman said. "And when we get through with that program, I don't think there will be any doubt about the result."[10]

The next morning, Truman hopped aboard the seventeen-car *Ferdinand Magellan*, a specially equipped luxury train.[11] They headed toward the Midwest at 80 mph, the breakneck speed a metaphor for his entire presidential campaign. The first stops would be in Iowa, before heading west. His itinerary seemed appropriate, for the odds of winning the election "loomed as large as the Rocky Mountains," wrote Marquis Childs, one of the seventy reporters on Truman's train.[12] Elmo Roper, one of the nation's most respected pollsters, had suspended his work because he considered the election essentially over.[13] The Gallup Poll had Truman trailing Dewey by ten points among farm voters, an embarrassing development for a farmer-president who took pride in his plowing ability.[14]

The Staley Milling Company of Kansas City also conducted a poll that autumn. As farmers came into their feed stores, they were asked to buy an elephant-labeled feed bag if they were support-ing Dewey or a donkey-labeled feed bag if they were supporting Truman.[15] President Truman's strategists believed he could not win without the farm vote.[16] He had a lot of ground to make up and only forty-seven days to close the gap.

On September 18, 1948, at 8:50 a.m., the *Ferdinand Magellan* rolled into Oxford, Iowa.[17] With the presidential seal fixed to the rear platform and three loudspeakers mounted on the roof, Truman gave his third speech of the day, an appeal for rural voters in the crucial swing state.

"I don't have to convince you about conservation and crop insurance and rural electrification and those other things which the Democratic Party instituted and which have given the farmers the greatest prosperity they have had in their history."

Then it was on to Dexter, Iowa, to a massive crowd of seventy-five thousand.[18] Reporter Childs recalled the speech as one of the most important of the campaign. "To the huge crowd of farmers who had come miles around in their shiny new cars Truman recited the farm benefits flowing from the New Deal and the Fair Deal, including rural electrification."

Truman was executing his plan, but ignoring his opponents was a unique strategy by any measure of a presidential campaign. Dewey's name was never uttered.[19] Nor were the fellow Democrats who had splintered off to run on third-party tickets. Former Vice President Henry Wallace ran on the Progressive Party ticket while South Carolina Governor Strom Thurmond was in the race as a Dixiecrat, running on the platform of states' rights. (Thurmond later became a Republican U.S. Senator and champion of rural electrification, often campaigning at co-op annual meetings.) Truman acted as though his opponent in the 1948 election was the Republican-controlled 80th Congress.

They were, for Truman, a "Do-Nothing" Congress. A minority party in the House since 1931, the Republicans had read their mandate after their 1946 takeover as a repudiation of the New Deal. Truman used his veto pen and constantly outmaneuvered them. The Republicans were doing nothing in Truman's estimation for rural electrification. Earlier that year, Truman had requested $175 million in additional REA funding, but the U.S. House Appropriations Committee granted only $75 million.[20] When Democrats forced a vote to increase REA funding, most Republicans voted no. Whenever his train crossed into electric co-op territory, Truman was going to remind voters in his own unique way about who supported rural electrification.

Texas was definitely co-op country, and Truman brought Sam Rayburn and Senate candidate Lyndon Johnson on the train to bolster his message.[21] LBJ had defeated his Senate primary opponent by eighty-seven votes using REA as one of his campaign planks. Truman's stem-winder campaign speech in Bonham, Texas, was one of the few broadcast to a national radio audience.[22]

> Ask Sam Rayburn how many of the big money boys helped, when he was sweating blood to get electricity for farmers and the people in the small towns . . . There have been six record votes in Congress on the REA. In all but one of those record votes, only about 12 to 25 percent of the Republicans voted in favor of the REA . . . I am deeply concerned about what the Republicans would do to the rural electrification program if they could get control of the whole government.[23]

The speech was a preview of things to come. That autumn, Truman took his rural electrification message to places hard to find on a map, but places that would help decide close elections: Mount Vernon, Illinois; Genoa, New York; Richmond, Indiana; and Keyer, West Virginia. Truman's speeches often invoked violent imagery. In Shawnee, Oklahoma, Truman said, *"The cuts they made put the ax to your program of rural electrification."*[24] Eleven hours later, in Seminole, Oklahoma, he said, *"They tried to tear up the rural electrification program."*

Of course, it was not a single-issue campaign.[25] Targeting his locale and audience, Truman spoke of labor issues in Detroit, mining policy in Denver, and ranching in Texas. He would lambaste the Republicans for the high cost of living, failing to vote for grain-storage bins, and for slashing federal support for hydroelectric power projects in California. (During a stop in Los Angeles, a liberal Democrat actor named Ronald Reagan appeared at Truman's campaign event.) As historian David McCullough observed, "He just kept pressing the attack, mindful always of where he was and to whom he was speaking."

Truman hammered the Republican Congress before audiences that were often larger than the entire town's population. Someone would usually shout from the crowd, "Give 'em hell, Harry!"[26] This brought laughter and yells of approval, especially when Truman ridiculed the 80th Congress. "I never gave anybody hell," Truman would later say. "I just told them the truth and they thought it was hell."

In mid-October, President Truman was in Minnesota, a battleground state he had to win.[27] Truman had not gone to bed until after midnight, but on October 15, he was up early for a walk on a crisp fall morning in Mankato. The crowd was already assembling. Just after 8 a.m., more than five thousand people surrounded the rear platform of the train. Campaigning with Hubert Humphrey, a candidate for the U.S. Senate and a strong advocate for electric co-ops, Truman delivered in rapid-fire fashion his most comprehensive speech on the REA.

> Now, thanks to REA and the great work done by farmer cooperatives since then, six out of every ten Minnesota farms has electricity—and we're going to get those other four before we get through. But in order to do that, you've got to vote for yourselves. You've got to put somebody in the White House and somebody in Congress that will look after your interests . . . No one here doubts that cooperatives are a good thing. They have been a tremendous boon to the farmer.[28]

Enthralled, the Minnesotans cheered when Truman discussed the REA and co-ops.[29] They cheered louder when he introduced his wife, Bess, and their daughter, Margaret, the crowd showering them with bouquets of roses. A headline the next day in the *Minneapolis*

Star announced TRUMAN RAPS OPPONENTS ON CO-OP POLICY.
Another headline declared: STATE PLANS 'BIGGEST DEWEY RALLY.'

Dewey was coming to Minnesota because something was happening among the electorate; the Republicans sensed that Truman's
message was resonating with rural voters. A Minnesota congressman implored Dewey to address the discontent among farmers.[30]
"We cannot win without the farm vote," he wrote. At Staley Milling
Company stores, donkey-labeled feed bags were selling at an unusually brisk pace for a candidate who had no chance to win.

Dewey was worried. In St. Paul, he reminded his audience that the Republican Congress "had voted by far the largest
amount ever provided by any Congress to speed electricity to our
farms—$800,000,000."

On November 2, 1948, the campaign was over. Dewey had conducted a cautious, hold-the-ball campaign while Truman had sought
out every voter in the small towns of America, delivering an amazing
337 speeches. He had given his all, but it was not enough. The final
Gallup poll showed Truman trailing Dewey by five points.[31]

On election night, as the nation waited on edge for the results,
Harry Truman went to sleep.[32] In the following hours, the returns
came in showing Democrats doing unusually well. Awaking at
midnight, Truman flipped on the radio to learn that he was ahead
by two million votes.[33] However, NBC newsman H.V. Kaltenborn
still did not see how Truman could win because the rural vote in key
states, such as Ohio and Illinois, had not been counted. Truman's
friend Tom Evans called him and told him that New York had gone
for Dewey and that he would need Ohio, Illinois, and California.[34]

"Tom, I am going back to sleep," Truman told Evans. "Now don't
call me anymore. I am going to carry all three of those states."

And Truman was right. The next morning, Thomas Dewey
conceded defeat. Harry Truman had pulled off the biggest upset

in presidential history.[35] He carried twenty-eight states with a total
of 303 electoral votes, defeating Dewey by more than two million
votes. A patchwork coalition of labor, African Americans and
Westerners helped him win, but success in rural areas was instru-
mental to his victory.[36] Author David Pietrusza summed up the
campaign in his book *1948*, "It came down to so many factors: an
underdog who refused to surrender, a presumed victor who refused
to fight . . . and fearful Republican farmers who, in the end, proved
more farmers than Republican.[37]

Farmers helped Truman trounce Dewey in Minnesota by more
than two hundred thousand votes.[38] Almost every place where
Truman spoke about rural electrification, he won. He carried Iowa
and Illinois and of the eight largest corn-producing states, he won
six. While the Gallup and Roper polling companies were stunned by
the results, the Staley Milling Company had seen it coming.[39]

It may not have been scientific, but on election eve, Truman
led Dewey among farmers at their feed stores 54 to 46 percent.
Historian Zachary Karabell wrote, "The man who would be elected
by no small measure by the farm vote won the only poll dominated
by farmers." A Truman supporter later sent the president a donkey
feed bag as a tribute to his efforts.

To this day, the most iconic image of the 1948 campaign is
the photo of Truman holding up the early morning edition of the
Chicago Tribune that read DEWEY DEFEATS TRUMAN. But the real
story for electric co-ops was the clout they now brought to the
American political scene. Harry Truman's appearance before the
NRECA regional meeting was no accident. His instinct told him it
was good policy and good politics to go all out for the rural electric
program. REA funding and federal hydroelectric projects were
defining issues in some parts of the country, helping change the
course of American electoral history.

Yet how Harry Truman prevailed in the 1948 election continues to be a rich topic for political scientists to this day. For Tom Dewey, the question was moot. "The farm vote switched in the last ten days," he wrote in a letter, "and you can analyze figures from now to kingdom come and all they will show is that we lost the farm vote . . ."[40]

Clyde Ellis seized the moment.[41] He immediately sent a telegram congratulating Truman. He also asked for a meeting. If Truman had any notion to refuse, Ellis concluded the telegram with a postscript: HOW DID YOU LIKE THAT FARM VOTE FOR A CHANGE?

Less than a month after the election, Ellis was in the Oval Office.

He brought a wish list of items: more funding for REA personnel, accelerated farm research, and authorization of REA funds for telephone service.[42] But it was Truman's strong support of federal hydroelectric projects that created much of his legacy. Hydropower was an increasingly important source of electricity for electric co-ops, particularly in the West. It was also good politics. Truman once noted that he "dedicated the Grand Coulee Dam two or three times" on a "nonpolitical tour" across the country.[43]

Truman may have lacked FDR's eloquence and grand vision for rural electrification, but he made up for it with passion and a disdain for the big power companies that continued to fight electric co-ops. Philip Voltz, an employee of TVA and REA during the Truman administration, remembers talking to Truman after the president gave a speech to a group of rural electric leaders.[44] Truman held up an ad from a power company and told Voltz he was going to have the attorney general investigate them. "And for the first time," Voltz said, "I heard the president use words which probably wouldn't be permitted on TV or even on tape today."

Barry Hart, CEO of the Association of Missouri Electric Cooperatives, believes "Truman's strong support for electric co-ops stemmed not only from being born in a farmhouse with no electricity, but because of his close friendship with local electric co-op managers in the early days of his political career."[45] These electric co-op managers, like Truman, had no idea he would be president, but it was their job to engage elected officials. Truman never forgot their support.

If Harry Truman was one of the unlikeliest men to occupy the Oval Office, Ellis knew where he would rank. Truman, he said, was a "terrific man, a genuine diamond in the rough . . . I am sure that history will finally render the judgment that he was one of our greatest presidents."[46]

———— • ◆ • ————

On his final day in office, Truman again boarded the *Ferdinand Magellan*, a courtesy from President Eisenhower so Truman could return to his Missouri home.[47] Truman, a man who never wanted to be president, had helped create an America where 85 percent of the farms had electricity. Electric co-ops would miss him. They had enjoyed the support of two presidents who had championed the REA. Now, Clyde Ellis had to come to terms with a new reality.[48] President Dwight D. Eisenhower was a man of remarkable achievement, but he had spent more time drawing up invasion plans for Normandy than promoting rural electrification.

During the 1952 campaign, candidate Eisenhower had, at least, said the right things. "We must always be concerned with strengthening farmer cooperatives which have done so much . . . developing rural electrification and telephone service."[49] In winning the White House, Eisenhower carried all but nine of the forty-eight states and had cracked FDR's Democratic coalition, winning rural and suburban voters.

The power companies also sensed a new political opportunity. "It seemed impossible to pick up any national magazine without seeing a power company ad blasting every kind of federal participation in the electric power business," Ellis wrote.[50] The TVA was often a prime target of the power companies. By the late 1950s, it became clear electric co-ops needed their own generating and transmission (G & T) capacity to meet their power supply needs, but they found little help from the Eisenhower administration.

Electric co-ops were maturing as political and marketing entities, maintaining scorecards on legislators and rolling out an official mascot named Willie Wiredhand. But they were never able to win over Eisenhower.

By 1959, the relationship between electric co-ops and Eisenhower was on shaky ground. "Eisenhower just never did seem to comprehend what the rural electrification program was all about," wrote Ellis.[51] The president, Ellis added, "was frequently irritated that what he regarded as an obscure program could be a source of controversy."

This controversy centered on the REA 2 percent loan program. In 1959, with nearly 96 percent of the country electrified, the Eisenhower administration argued that the nation could no longer afford REA in its current form.[52] NRECA disagreed, contending that the capital requirements for an electric system were so tremendous that many co-ops could not survive if the rate was higher than 2 percent.

In February 1959, NRECA invited Eisenhower to make his case in Washington, D.C., before the largest gathering of co-op leaders in the history of the rural electric program. What occurred after that, neither NRECA nor Dwight D. Eisenhower would ever forget.

President Dwight D. Eisenhower at the 1959 NRECA Annual Meeting in Washington, D.C. While waiting for his speech, Eisenhower said, "My God, what a crowd." The speech led to an epic legislative fight between NRECA and the Eisenhower administration.

3

D-DAY FOR REA

"Ours is not a wealthy program and we have never been able to match the financial resources of our opponents. But rural electrification is a people's program, and people vote, and they influence the votes of others . . ."[1]

FORMER NRECA GENERAL MANAGER CLYDE T. ELLIS

O N FEBRUARY 11, 1959, PRESIDENT DWIGHT D. EISENHOWER and his press secretary, James Hagerty, left the White House in a motorcade for a short ride to the Washington, D.C., Armory.[2] It is uncertain what they discussed going up Pennsylvania Avenue, but chances are it involved, for the president at least, a sense of unease.

There were more than seven thousand electric co-op leaders anxiously awaiting his message on the future of REA,[3] massed together like the giant army he had commanded in Europe. Clyde Ellis had already delivered an explosive one hundred-minute speech, accusing the Eisenhower administration of being "hell bent on handing us over to the Wall Street bankers." If that wasn't enough to make the president believe he was entering a lion's den, U.S. Senate

Majority Leader Lyndon Johnson had also appeared. He had urged co-op leaders in his bellowing, gesticulating style[4] to "fight with beer bottles if necessary" to protect the REA 2 percent loan program.

That Eisenhower was in the motorcade at all required an unusual chain of events. The White House staff initially declined Ellis's offer for the president to speak, as Eisenhower confidante Wilton Persons told aides to "politely" turn down NRECA's invitation.[5] But U.S. Agriculture Secretary Ezra Benson intervened, strongly urging the president to reconsider. It would be an excellent opportunity, Benson argued, to set the record straight in front of an audience that "have been charging repeatedly" that the administration was "trying to kill off REA."[6] Benson also noted that administration spokesmen had, in the past, been "courteously received." A back-channel message was sent to NRECA: Invite the president again. This time, Eisenhower accepted.

Ellis accommodated the White House, for he knew the speech would make history.[7] It would be the first time a sitting president had ever addressed an NRECA annual meeting, and Eisenhower would be an unlikely chief executive to hold that distinction. FDR had died before he could keep his commitment to Ellis, and Truman had only attended the smaller, regional meeting before the 1948 Whistle-stop campaign. Eisenhower deserved credit for showing up, even if he didn't want to be there.

It was a pivotal time in the Eisenhower presidency. Eisenhower was sixty-eight years old, a month removed from a year he'd called the worst of his life.[8] A year in which he suffered a stroke, watched powerlessly as the country slipped into a recession, and Republicans get drubbed in the mid-term elections. Now as he approached the hulking Armory, there was Ellis waiting for him at the curb. Earlier in the day, Eisenhower had met with the Boy Scouts.[9] The electric co-ops were not going to be as easy.

The president greeted Ellis and they warily strolled into the Armory, along with NRECA Board President John George. They headed inside to what, on its surface, was just another Washington, D.C., trade association event, one of scores that are held each year, a meeting planner's juggling act of hotels and high-profile speakers to entertain dues-paying members.

The 1959 NRECA Annual Meeting was more akin to a block-buster political convention, both for the intensity of the issues and the absolute firepower on the program. The agenda featured a sitting president, two future presidents—John F. Kennedy and Lyndon Johnson—and one of the most powerful legislators of any era, U.S. House Speaker Sam Rayburn.

Moreover, it marked the largest meeting ever of electric co-op leaders and their first annual meeting held in the nation's capital. A rare convergence of policy and personalities, the event was set against the backdrop of a president attempting to regain the initiative and the first stirrings of the 1960 Democratic presidential primary. But the combustible dynamics between President Eisenhower and Clyde Ellis nearly overshadowed this high drama and political intrigue.

Eisenhower bristled at Ellis's relentless in-your-face advocacy.[10] Eisenhower's Chief of Staff Sherman Adams had one concern when he first interviewed David Hamil for the job of REA administrator. "Can you handle this man Ellis?" Adams asked.[11]

For his part, Ellis believed Eisenhower was letting his staff kill REA. Electric co-ops had watched their REA loan applications languish, and there was substantial evidence that Secretary Benson rejected loans that were not supported by the large power companies.[12] This secret policy was leading to another potential showdown as NRECA crafted legislation with U.S. Senator Hubert Humphrey and U.S. Representative Mel Price to block the politicization of REA loans.[13]

As the crowd waited for the Marine Corps Band to play "Hail to the Chief," Ellis wondered which Eisenhower would show up at the podium.[14] Would it be the man who supported REA and TVA during his two campaigns, who had used a 1954 press conference to dispel the rumor that REA was on the chopping block? Or would it be the person who had allowed REA to be undermined by the big power companies? Did the president, Ellis also wondered, have the audacity to "attack the program to our faces?"

The meeting had become something else, too: an opportunity for Democratic presidential candidates to impress rural voters. Humphrey, one of the strongest electric co-op supporters on Capitol Hill, was scheduled to speak, but was stranded by a blizzard in Minneapolis. LBJ had already fired up the crowd.[15] He desperately wanted to be president, but would not get into the race, believing the other candidates would knock each other off in the primaries and he could win the nomination in the backroom. The man with the most to gain was a Massachusetts Senator with a spotty record on rural issues and who had just opened a presidential campaign office: John F. Kennedy.

Working behind the scenes, Kennedy aide Ted Sorensen plotted to have Kennedy seated on the stage at the same time as Eisenhower to rebut the administration's REA policy.[16] But Ellis vetoed the idea of a face-to-face debate between the two men. Kennedy was given a time slot later in the afternoon, and he would make the most of his opportunity.

President Eisenhower's speech was cloaked in mystery. Before being introduced, he stood on the edge of the stage, looking out at the 7,261 registered attendees. Every seat was filled. Banks of TV cameras crammed an elevated platform.

"My God," President Eisenhower remarked. "What a crowd."[17]

At 2:30 p.m., John George introduced Eisenhower. The president was warmly received, the applause echoing through the Armory. Eisenhower set his speech on a podium brimming with microphones. Recognizing that he had been pilloried by previous speakers, Eisenhower got right to the point.

"I understand there has been a little advance billing here about my alleged views on matters of interest to you," the president said.[18] He had underlined the sentence on the text for emphasis. "Well, I am here to set forth my views accurately and frankly, in what I believe to be your own interest as well as in the interest of the country." He then recited statistics to back up his assertion that the work of the REA was almost done.

"And today, of course, you know that 95 percent of our farms have central-station electric service. Your record of meeting loan repayments on time or ahead of schedule is outstanding . . . Much of this growth has taken place these past six years. Since January 1, 1953, you have added eight hundred thousand new consumers . . ."

It was a promising start, yet for electric co-op leaders, there was little of the fabled Eisenhower charm. White House speechwriters had toiled over the text, working to simplify it from a speech originally written for Agriculture Secretary Benson.[19] Relations between Benson and NRECA had deteriorated so badly that he wasn't even invited to the meeting. Nevertheless, it became clear to electric co-op leaders that even though Benson was absent, Eisenhower's speech reflected his animus toward the REA.

"America at this moment is engaged in a great debate on the role of the government in the lives of her citizens," the president said. "A part of this debate revolves around the question: shall government live within its means; shall our citizens, in prosperous times, meet the cost of the services they desire of the government."[20] The president's tone had turned cold and blunt.

"Now I come to the point on which I realize full well there is disagreement. Parenthetically, I feel obliged to say this: I believe we are not going to find decent solutions to any of these differences—or to any other serious problems facing our country—by resorting to demagoguery . . ."

President Eisenhower let the "demagoguery" accusation hang in the air. Who exactly he was referring to was not revealed until years later, but now he approached the central theme of his speech.

"One difference of which I speak of is the rate of interest paid by persons and agencies who borrow money from the Federal Treasury. Specifically, I refer to programs—such as REA and college housing—in which borrowers do not pay interest rates equal to the cost of money to the government and are capable of doing so."

Ellis waited with anticipation. Then Eisenhower dropped a bombshell. *"I have recommended that the Congress authorize the Treasury to set these rates at a level that will recover the cost of money loaned."*

Just as electric co-op leaders had feared, the president of the United States had called for a doubling of the REA interest rate, an action many believed would devastate the rural electric program. Not far from the podium, Ellis fumed.[21] Eisenhower, he thought, read the speech "as a teacher would talk to a group of errant schoolboys. He was trying to shame the co-op people into agreeing that it was morally wrong to borrow government money, and wrong to pay the 2 percent interest provided by law."

Eisenhower had made his point and there was no reason to prolong his speech. He believed that any speaker lost the crowd after more than ten minutes, and he was fast approaching that deadline. He crossed out a significant paragraph from the text dealing with private financing proposals. The White House said later there was "no particular reason" why the paragraph was dropped.[22]

President Eisenhower concluded, receiving polite applause when he told the co-ops that their program, "which lighted the farm homes of America, will also help illuminate the path to sound finance, good government, and responsible citizenship."[23] And then he was quickly escorted out of the Armory. He was on the South Lawn putting green before electric co-op leaders could assess the ramifications of what they had just heard.[24]

They had been in the presence of a genuine American hero, but they had also witnessed the first direct attack from a U.S. president on the REA. They had heard an eight-minute speech read with little emotion from a president who appeared as though he wanted to be someplace else. However, the marker had been laid down. In a matter of weeks, electric co-ops would be forced into legislative battle against a president who had spent a lifetime winning battles.

———— • ❖ • ————

In the immediate aftermath of his speech, Eisenhower closely followed the press coverage of the NRECA meeting, learning that electric co-op leaders—not surprisingly—had rejected his recommendation to increase the REA interest rate. He was also irritated that Kennedy had endeared himself to co-op leaders with a stirring repudiation of the administration's policies.

"You are not the recipients of some federal charity," Kennedy had said.[25] According to *The New York Times*, he'd been interrupted by applause seven times while Eisenhower's reception was "cool." Kennedy may have won the day inside the Armory, but outside, Eisenhower was easily winning the public relations battle.

The White House media office aggressively pushed Eisenhower's message on the REA "subsidy," inspiring a raft of editorials in

newspapers across the nation in favor of its position.[26] The stack of
negative press clippings on Ellis's desk made it clear that round one
in the fight was a knockout for the administration. "Ike's speech
made the issue," Ellis wrote, "and the commentators and editors
made it echo and reecho everywhere."

Then things became personal. After Benson congratulated
Eisenhower on his speech, the president quickly responded with a
note that revealed his true feelings toward Ellis.

> **I do not particularly enjoy being cast in the role of debating
> with a *pipsqueak* whose job is little more than that of a lobbyist.
> However, he does seem to be a successful one, since I see from
> the paper that the convention rejected my recommendation by
> a unanimous vote.[27]**

Being called a "pipsqueak" by President Eisenhower may have
been a badge of honor for Ellis. However, petty name-calling took
a back seat to the emerging legislative fight on Capitol Hill. If
Eisenhower had prevailed in round one of the battle, electric co-ops
were winning round two in Congress. The Humphrey-Price legislation (S. 144), which gave the REA administrator final approval over
loan applications, sailed through both the House and Senate. As
expected, Eisenhower vetoed the bill with a sharp rebuke, setting
up a bitter override fight that had all the makings of a Hollywood
political thriller.

NRECA's political muscle was being tested as never before.
Battling the big power companies seemed like an everyday activity,
but never had electric co-op leaders squared off against a popular
president. They had prepared for this day, fostering relations on
both sides of the political aisle. Letters poured in from across
the country.[28] NRECA's success in Congress was predicated on

maintaining overwhelming Democratic support and holding the handful of Republicans who had voted with them and against the president the first time. It was a tall order; no one doubted the outcome was going to be close.

The Senate prepared to vote on April 28, 1959. Few legislators were better at corralling votes than LBJ, but he needed help. During the Senate debate to override the president's veto, he called Ellis. Without any small talk, Johnson said, "We need more votes from the Republicans. Good-bye."[29] Despite a flurry of phone calls from Eisenhower and Benson to wavering Senators, Ellis found the votes. Senator Frank Church of Idaho even received special clearance from the Federal Aviation Administration to land early to vote for NRECA's position. NRECA helped override Eisenhower's veto in the Senate with two votes to spare.

U.S. Senator Everett Dirksen, the Republican leader, saw larger implications for the override.[30] If powerful outside organizations like NRECA, Dirksen said, could pass the rural electrification bill, then other organizations in other fields would do the same thing. The consequence, Dirksen believed, would be to "whittle down" the authority of Cabinet members such as Benson.

The fight now turned to the U.S. House of Representatives on April 30. Both sides targeted the sixteen Republican congressmen who had voted with NRECA the first time. Would they remain loyal to electric co-ops and vote to override the veto, or would they switch and align with the president? Benson pressed hard for their votes. "This was more than the struggle over REA, it would undoubtedly influence the future course of the administration," Benson wrote.[31]

The votes at first appeared to be holding for electric co-ops. Eisenhower needed a game-changing move to peel off the sixteen Republican votes, and he found it with the American Farm Bureau.[32]

Though the Farm Bureau had previously shown no interest in the issue, they came out against the override as a favor to the president.

It was a blatantly political act, but it was a brilliant tactical move that NRECA could not counter. With a farm group in their corner, rural Republicans now could stand with the administration. Electric co-ops saw their support suddenly evaporate, and they scrambled for a majority. U.S. Representative Jaime Whitten, a Mississippi Democrat, got out of his sickbed against doctor's orders to support NRECA. Republican U.S. Representative H. Carl Anderson left Bethesda Naval Hospital to vote for the override. But when the gavel came down in the House chamber, NRECA had fallen four votes short.

Eisenhower was overjoyed. "We were like a couple of kids celebrating a hard-fought football game," Benson wrote.[33] It was a bitter loss for NRECA. Ellis called it a "black Thursday for us, even though we knew our best efforts had come within a four-vote margin of beating down what the United Press International called 'party discipline of a kind that is rarely seen on Capitol Hill.'"

Republican U.S. Representative Gerald R. Ford of Michigan voted against the override and with Eisenhower, but he knew it was a razor-thin victory. "The president won, but . . . both sides are tightening their belts for the next round," he wrote.[34]

There was no next round. Eisenhower's proposal to double the REA interest rate went nowhere, creating a split decision between the White House and NRECA. By 1960, they were like two bloodied prizefighters who had no interest in a rematch. Yet, Eisenhower seemed invigorated and, curiously, his speech before NRECA took on a life of its own.

In 1960, *Time Magazine* honored Eisenhower as its "Man of the Year." In a glowing profile, the magazine lauded his message of fiscal austerity in a "little noticed 1959 speech" to a "hostile audience" gathered in Washington, D.C., "to holler it up for continued government subsidy of rural electrification."[35]

Ironically, a speaking invitation the White House had initially declined became a centerpiece of Eisenhower's campaign for fiscal discipline. And a speech that President Eisenhower didn't even deliver as written helped land him on the cover of one of the nation's most prestigious magazines. Ellis looked at the 1960 election as a way to put behind "the terrible years of Eisenhower. We didn't want any more of it," he said.[36] But their paths would cross again.

Interestingly, after leaving office, Eisenhower took up residence at his Gettysburg, Pennsylvania, farm in an area served by Adams Electric Cooperative. Started in 1940, Adams Electric received its first REA loan that year, constructing its system despite opposition by the local private power companies. It was on his farm that Eisenhower wrote his book, *Mandate for Change*, published in 1963, where he recounted the fateful NRECA Annual Meeting and how he told electric co-op leaders that "they could no longer live at the expense of other taxpayers."[37] Eisenhower was incredulous at the crowd's reaction. "The opposition hit the roof," he wrote.

He also pointed a not-so-subtle finger at Ellis. "And year after year, the general manager of the National Rural Electric Cooperative Association, the lobbying organization of REA, unveiled bits and pieces of an alleged top secret administration 'master plan,' which he alone had discovered, to wreck REA." He also made a forceful case for his record on federal hydropower production, rebutting President Truman's contention that "only the Democratic Party could produce power progress."

Eisenhower lived out his final years at the farm, even appearing at the Adams Electric Cooperative twenty-fifth anniversary at the local Holiday Inn. The keynote speaker for the business meeting was Clyde Ellis. However, there was no confrontation. Eisenhower shook hands with co-op directors and one of the political giants of the electric co-op program, William Matson, the general manager of the Pennsylvania Rural Electric Association.[38] The men talked about cattle, and Eisenhower departed before the celebration dinner.

The Eisenhower saga came full circle in 2011 when Eisenhower's granddaughter Susan, a well-regarded energy expert, spoke to the 69th NRECA Annual Meeting in Orlando, Florida. In addition to discussing America's energy future, she professed admiration for electric co-ops. "Actually, this movement, of course, is the closest of all to the consumers of electricity in the country," she said.[39]

She made no mention of her grandfather's speech to electric co-op leaders more than fifty years before. There was, however, one similarity. Like her grandfather, she was courteously received.

After that February day in the Armory in 1959, Eisenhower expressed disappointment with John F. Kennedy's speech and "felt it a pity that he did not follow the advice of a great Democratic leader of yesteryear and say, 'Let's look at the record.'"[40] Eisenhower's speech may have helped land him *Time Magazine's* Man of the Year, but Kennedy's refusal to concede the rural vote to his primary challengers played a crucial role in his presidential campaign.

In 1960, rural America was changing. Rural electrification celebrated its twenty-fifth anniversary. More than four million consumers were members of electric co-ops, and the numbers were growing rapidly in the postwar boom.

On Inauguration Day in January 1961, John F. Kennedy was sworn in as the thirty-fifth president of the United States. In his inaugural speech, the young, handsome president told the world "we shall pay any price, bear any burden, meet any hardship, support any friend, oppose any foe to assure the survival and the success of liberty." Soon, those words would be put to the test, and electric co-ops would be given an entirely different mission.

In November 1962, in the immediate aftermath of the Cuban Missile Crisis, President Kennedy looked to America's electric co-ops to bear the burden of one of his most pressing international goals: to stop more dictators like Fidel Castro from rising up in Latin America.

Clyde Ellis signs NRECA-U.S. AID contract in the Oval Office on November 1, 1962.
Minutes later, President John F. Kennedy was again working on the Cuban Missile Crisis.

4

THE POLES AND
WIRES OF NOVEMBER

IF SUCH A THING AS A NORMAL MORNING EXISTED AT THE
White House, President John F. Kennedy usually started it with
breakfast in his bedroom and a stack of newspapers and secret
diplomatic cables delivered during the night. Somehow he was able
to focus, despite the cartoons blaring in the background for the
entertainment of his young children, John and Caroline.[1] For the
previous three weeks, events had been far from normal. The early
morning routines most families took for granted—breakfast, the
morning paper, and cartoons—were, for a period of days, at risk
from nuclear annihilation.

In October 1962, President Kennedy was informed of a U-2
spy-plane's discovery of Soviet nuclear-tipped missiles in Cuba. The
nuclear strike force could reach most major U.S. cities in less than
five minutes.[2] The president decided immediately that the Soviet
Union's actions could not be tolerated. Over an intense thirteen
days, the world held its breath as Kennedy and his Russian counter-
part Nikita Khrushchev confronted each other in a diplomatic chess
match, each with the power of mutual destruction. A nuclear war

would have meant the deaths of one hundred million Americans and more than one hundred million Russians.

On Sunday, October 28, Khrushchev agreed to remove the missiles from Cuba, culminating what Kennedy aide Ted Sorensen called the "most dangerous thirteen days in the history of the mankind."[3] Kennedy, by all measures, had showed determination and courage under pressure, ignoring recommendations by his military advisers for an invasion of Cuba. Many believed it was Kennedy's finest hour as president. Yet the hour was not over.

On November 1, 1962, *The New York Times* headline read: CASTRO IS BALKING AT INSPECTION; MISSILE REMOVAL ON, U.N. HEARS. U.S. RENEWS AIR-SEA WATCH TODAY.

President Kennedy had other secret information, including a U.S. State Department cable that arrived after midnight. "Castro in impossible and bitter mood. He was extremely bitter at soviets . . ."[4]

While the almost unbearable international tension of the Cuban Missile Crisis may have abated, it still continued. Tens of thousands of Soviet troops were still deployed in Cuba, as well as Soviet nuclear submarines.[5] New tensions quickly mounted between the United States and the Soviet Union over inspection of missile sites and the withdrawal of other deadly short-range weapons. The crisis was ongoing.

Reflecting this volatile situation, the president cleared his schedule except for the most pressing meetings. This included a 10 a.m. meeting with an ad hoc group called the Executive Committee, or ExComm, which advised him throughout the missile crisis.[6] The ExComm included, among others, Secretary of State Dean Rusk, Defense Secretary Robert McNamara, and the president's brother, Bobby Kennedy, the nation's attorney general.

Only one other meeting, an unusual one, was scheduled the entire day, at 9:30 a.m. It was a routine contract signing that rarely involves the president. This type of event, in this case between the U.S. Agency for International Development (USAID) and NRECA, typically occurs with little fanfare in the stale confines of a federal office building. Yet, there was nothing routine about what Kennedy had experienced in the previous days. There were many reasons that, at the appointed hour, Kennedy was in the Oval Office waiting for electric co-op leaders. It had to do with politics, diplomacy, and a bottle of wine.

———————— • ◆ • ————————

If it was an unlikely meeting in the most dangerous of times, it was also between unlikely allies. On the day Jack Kennedy was born, his father was named to the board of the Massachusetts Electric Company, an investor-owned utility.[7] Unlike Vice President Lyndon Johnson, who had watched his mother grow stooped-shouldered lugging buckets of water from a well, Kennedy's family was one of the richest in America. But to lay claim to the family's ultimate prize of the U.S. presidency, Kennedy also needed electric co-ops.

Until 1956, when Kennedy decided to run for national office, his voting record on electric co-op issues was less than stellar.[8] Then he became a convert, taking notes at an NRECA Board of Directors meeting in a room adorned with photographs of electric co-op heroes such as George Norris and Sam Rayburn. Even though Kennedy had challenged Eisenhower at the Armory in 1959, he still had acres of ground to make up in the 1960 Democratic primary as his main rival, Hubert Humphrey of Minnesota, was a militant electric co-op supporter.

Kennedy slogged through the snow during the Wisconsin primary in February 1960, taking direct aim at the rural electrification policy of the Eisenhower-Nixon administration. "Instead of reducing REA loans, we should be increasing them," Kennedy told a crowd in Antigo. "Instead of trying to increase REA interest rates, we should keep them where they are."[9] His victory in Wisconsin ended Humphrey's chances for the Democratic nomination.

John Kennedy's transformation from urban legislator to a champion of rural America was remarkable, if not politically expedient. Former NRECA CEO Glenn English believed he had no choice. "Electric co-ops were a national power. JFK knew we were important," English said. "It was a recognition that co-op managers would call out elected officials at their annual meetings if they were not supportive."[10]

After Kennedy won the Democratic Party nomination in 1960, Ellis made his strongest political statement for any presidential ticket since he had joined NRECA.[11] Concluding that another anti-rural electrification White House "would be fatal," Ellis convinced NRECA's membership to join the "Farmers for Kennedy" organization. Then the politics of rural electrification and the Electoral College collided.

Kennedy won a narrow victory over Richard Nixon in the 1960 presidential election, but the Democrat ran poorly in rural states with strong REA programs or in states that relied on federal hydropower, such as the Farm Belt and the Pacific Northwest.[12] Despite the efforts of electric co-op leaders, small town America was still not sold on JFK.

"The cadence and Harvard prose of John F. Kennedy, the meticulous grammar and elegance of the Democrat's style, were to such people alien and suspect," wrote author Theodore White.[13]

Kennedy's lack of support in REA country frustrated him. As Ellis and other NRECA leaders entered the Oval Office that morning of November 1, 1962, new hydropower programs were a sticking point in their relationship. Ellis had met with Kennedy the year before, claiming, in his usual blunt style, that the administration's hydropower program was "on dead center."[14] Kennedy promised action, but for Ellis, it seemed to get lost in the bureaucracy.

This Oval Office meeting, however, was about something more urgent than hydropower. It was about beginning the diplomatic repair work in Latin America as a result of the Cuban Missile Crisis. According to Ellis, President Kennedy had stirred the hopes of the Latin people as "no American had done" since FDR.[15] Yet, the United States' reputation in Latin America was in tatters.

Many Latinos looked upon the United States as a counter-revolutionary bully that favored right-wing dictatorships.[16] As historian Arthur Schlesinger noted, "If the United States were not ready to offer an affirmative program of democratic modernization, new Castros would undoubtedly rise across the continent. This was the nature of the crisis."[17]

Kennedy understood the political significance of electric co-ops and the diplomatic role they could play in Latin America. His own program, the Alliance for Progress, was designed to check the spread of communism by providing social and economic assistance to the region.[18] Rural electrification fit that mission. Work was already under way to share the lessons learned in rural America with developing countries around the world. Ellis called it "export-ing the REA pattern."[19]

NRECA had negotiated a contract with the USAID, establishing a partnership between the two entities to carry the electric co-op model to distant lands.[20] The stage had been set at an earlier meeting when Ellis had brought Kennedy a bottle of fine wine from a co-op leader in Peru.[21] Touched by the gesture, Kennedy asked that the contract signing be moved to the Oval Office. Instead of an obscure event at the State Department, the Oval Office now overflowed

with electric co-op leaders and administration officials, including
Secretary of Agriculture Orville Freeman and USAID administrator
Fowler Hamilton.

Kennedy's Oval Office reflected a president steeped in naval
tradition. Maritime paintings hung on the walls. Behind an oaken
shipboard desk made of timbers from the old *USS Resolute*,
Kennedy read an opening statement:

> **One of the most significant contributions we can make to the
> under-developed countries is to pass on to them the techniques
> which we in this country have developed and used successfully.
> It seems to me, therefore, that the contract signed today holds
> special promise for these countries that have only realized a
> small fraction of their energy potential. I express the hope
> that the results of the contract will be an improved standard of
> living for millions of people.[22]**

President Kennedy was under intense pressure and in perpetual
pain. Some believe he may have spent a second term in a wheelchair.
Nevertheless, he appeared relaxed and engaged as he discussed the
history of rural electrification, the clipped Boston accent coming
through as farm became "fawm."

Leaning back in his chair, Kennedy played the role of the jour-
nalist he had been in a former life, asking USAID's Hamilton how
the initiative was going to proceed. Fowler remarked that rural electrification "would spread through the contagion of example, because
what these gentleman and ladies are going to take down to Latin
America in their heads is going to be a lot more important than
what government bureaucrats carry in their pockets . . ." Turning to
Ellis, the president asked the percentage of electrified farms when
REA began in the 1930s.

"About 10 percent, in 1935," Ellis answered. And how long a period, the president asked, before an appropriate change?

"Most of the work was done from 1946 until 1960," Ellis replied. "We electrified most of America's farms in a period of a little more than a decade." The president's interest was clearly piqued. "And what percentage is now electrified?"

"About 97 percent," Ellis replied.

Kennedy immediately saw the opportunity. "I think that figure, to go from 10 percent to 97 percent, as a result of this cooperative effort by the national government and REAs, and the local communities, and private industry, should be encouraging to countries which have even less than 10 percent today. It shows it can be done. I think this is going to be very helpful."

Concealing a sense of fatigue, the president watched intently as Ellis signed the contract, the culmination of years of effort establishing a new partnership. Electric co-op leaders left the Oval Office knowing the real work in Latin America was only beginning. But there was optimism. Rural electrification meant new allies and new opportunities. The missiles of October could become the poles and wires of November.

Ellis caught a cab outside the White House gates as Kennedy again confronted the situation in Cuba. At his meeting with the ExComm, the president authorized continued low-level reconnaissance flights over airfields and missile bases, deciding that no immediate retaliatory measures would be carried out if U.S. aircraft were shot down. Later, he instructed U.S. negotiators to stress the importance of obtaining verification, which he described as "essential."[23]

The next day Kennedy would speak to the nation and announce that Soviet missile bases in Cuba were being dismantled and that "progress is being made toward the restoration and peace in the

Caribbean."[24] Nevertheless, days later, on November 5, the president did not consider the crisis over. "We must operate on the presumption that the Russians may try again," he told Secretary McNamara.[25]

Following his meetings with electric co-op leaders and the ExComm on November 1, Kennedy attended an All-Saints Day mass. He had much ahead of him. The mid-term elections were approaching, and there were already 11,500 American military men stationed in Vietnam. While his prayers were his own, he had much to contemplate. If the Cuban Missile Crisis was Kennedy's finest hour as president, it was clear he was counting on electric co-ops to help make sure he didn't face an hour like that ever again.

———•◆•———

Kennedy also continued his work to provide electricity at home. New multi-purpose river projects and major transmission lines were on the drawing board. While the Kennedy administration could not meet Ellis's exacting standards for hydroelectric development, JFK's support of hydropower is almost unrivaled in the modern Democratic Party, which is now more likely to support dismantling dams than constructing new ones. Attending the dedication of South Dakota's Oahe Dam in 1962, JFK called electric co-ops "a happy middle ground between private enterprise and public cooperation." He added, "I don't want to see the United States second in space or in the development of power resources."[26]

Ellis kept pushing Kennedy to be first in water resource development. On September 23, 1963, he was back in the Oval Office with Alex Radin, the executive director of the American Public Power Association, the trade group for municipal utilities. They had sent the White House a detailed memo that noted, "Initiation of major power dams has been sparse." Nevertheless, they stood by the

President John F. Kennedy dedicates the Oahe Dam in 1962. In his speech,
President Kennedy said, "I don't want to see the United States second
in space or in the development of water resources."

fireplace and thanked the president for his support of public power
in the last election.

"It didn't do me much good in the West," Kennedy quipped.
Ellis and Radin pressed their case for a nationwide power grid and
left in a buoyant mood.[27] A second Kennedy term would be more
productive for hydropower and other initiatives, Ellis thought. The
first USAID loan to an electric cooperative abroad was ready for
signature. There was nothing they couldn't accomplish in the second
term. And the White House was working hard on winning that
second term. If Kennedy did not do well in the West, he needed to
carry Texas. There were tentative dates for a five-city visit to the state
in November.

The schedule placed Kennedy in Dallas on November 22, 1963.

———— • ◆ • ————

President Kennedy did not live to see the spectacular international accomplishments that grew from the partnership signed into action on November 1, 1962. The single electric cooperative being developed in Latin America when he was assassinated transformed into a global program that he could not imagine over fifty years later.

He never knew that more than one hundred million people in the world now receive electricity because of the NRECA-USAID partnership, in more than fifty countries. He never saw the schools, the clinics, and the quality of life that extended beyond Latin America to countries such as Yemen and South Sudan.[28] And he never heard Bolivia's Fernando Haderspock of Cooperativa Rural de Electrificacion (CRE) thank him at the fiftieth anniversary celebration for NRECA's International Programs in 2012. For CRE, an idea to export the REA pattern led to what is now the largest electric cooperative in the world, serving four hundred thousand members.

With the Cuban Missile Crisis staring him in the face, John Kennedy's brief session in the Oval Office with electric co-op leaders showed extraordinary long-range vision. Lyndon Johnson, the nation's new president, also had a grand vision for rural electrification abroad. And it would contribute to his undoing.

LBJ knew about rural electrification. His political career had been launched by his work with REA in the Texas Hill Country. No one can say how history would have changed if Lyndon Baines Johnson had taken the job of REA administrator in 1939. Instead, Johnson was elected to the U.S. Senate and partnered with NRECA on every major piece of legislation of importance to electric co-ops.

In 1963, Clyde Ellis said, "Lyndon B. Johnson will make a great president."

As president, Johnson opened up his White House to the NRECA Electric Cooperative Youth Tour, a program he inspired as a U.S. Senator during NRECA's Annual Meeting in 1957. He urged electric co-ops to "send youngsters to the nation's capital where they can actually see what the flag stands for and represents." The tradition of thousands of Youth Tour students visiting Washington, D.C., continues each June.

But in 1965, Johnson was particularly interested in NRECA's progress in establishing new co-ops not in rural America, but in rural Vietnam. LBJ was increasingly focused on Southeast Asia, and he had a compatriot in Clyde Ellis. The NRECA chief may have been memorialized later as "Mr. Rural Electrification," but he also revealed himself to be somewhat of a cold warrior. After traveling to Vietnam, Ellis wrote the president a March 30, 1965, letter proposing an extraordinary, almost clandestine, mission for America's electric co-ops.

"'The Viet Cong strike in the dark. They hide by day in the jungle patches; move mostly at night. They are scared of the light; the South Vietnamese are scared of the dark."[29] Ellis believed that "electric co-ops can be an important factor in instilling confidence of the Vietnamese in democratic institutions." He concluded with a bold assertion. "We can help you stabilize the government in Vietnam, I believe. We can help you win the sneak war, I am sure."

In the summer of 1965, Lyndon Johnson hosted electric co-op leaders at the White House and took them up on their offer.

Together, they were going to win the war in Southeast Asia.

President Lyndon B. Johnson announces the escalation of the Vietnam War during a press conference on July 28, 1965. He had first informed electric co-op leaders of his plans two weeks before in the Rose Garden. NRECA aided his effort in Vietnam.

5

THE TEXAS HILL
COUNTRY AND
VIETNAM

THE SUN STREAKED ACROSS THE UNDULATING SOUTH LAWN
as President Lyndon Johnson prepared to address his guests.[1]
At a towering, six-foot-four-inches tall, Johnson appeared on this
glorious midsummer evening of July 14, 1965, almost larger than life.

> I am very happy to welcome to this Rose Garden and the White
> House such a group of taxpaying, economy-building, enter-
> prising Americans. It doesn't surprise me to find Clyde Ellis
> bringing you in here at this hour of the day. Last month our
> doorbell rang one afternoon and when the policemen opened
> the gate, we found Clyde out there with seven hundred young
> people, just in time for dinner . . .[2]

Laughter filled the Rose Garden as President Johnson needled his
good friend, who along with forty-five NRECA directors, had been
admitted through the Southwest Gate as though they were political

royalty. LBJ reserved a special place for electric co-op leaders. It wasn't only because he'd help start a co-op in Texas, or that he and NRECA had fought together against Eisenhower's anti-REA policies. NRECA was in the Rose Garden because its membership had helped LBJ rout U.S. Senator Barry Goldwater in the 1964 presidential election.

NRECA had organized a group called "Rural Americans for Johnson-Humphrey," and actively campaigned for the ticket.[3] In his letter requesting the meeting, Ellis had pointed out that even Republican members of his board had supported LBJ. While Ellis carried the message of an election with "life-or-death" consequences for rural Americans, Goldwater self-destructed in rural areas by bashing REA and calling for the sale of TVA.

The result was a drubbing of epic proportions, eclipsed only by Roosevelt's 1936 landslide. NRECA touted its role in the victory, pointing out that in twenty-three states, the rural areas went more heavily for Johnson than the state as a whole. NRECA's analysis showed that Johnson carried 59 percent of the rural vote, a dramatic increase over JFK's total. Electric co-op leaders had been there for LBJ in his time of need, but in the summer of 1965, the president needed them more than ever.

Johnson understood history and the limitations of power. He knew that after the 1936 election FDR overreached, that "the purge" which started so publically that day in Barnesville had led to political disaster. Nevertheless, Johnson was destined to repeat history, believing his victory represented, according to biographer Robert Dallek, an "endorsement for his Great Society, the War on Poverty, and a tough, but not reckless, hold-the-line policy against any Communist advance, particularly in Vietnam."[4]

And it was South Vietnam that Johnson wanted to talk about on a sultry ninety-degree night in the nation's capital. Opposition to the Vietnam conflict had been growing after Operation Rolling

Thunder, an expanded U.S. bombing campaign against the North Vietnamese. And that summer, presidential assistant Bill Moyers was deeply worried about LBJ's psychological deterioration.[5]

The day's *New York Times* foreshadowed Johnson's private torment. "President Johnson has confirmed what most people realize—that the United States is faced with 'new and serious decisions' in meeting the challenge of Vietnam. Although it is not officially acknowledged, the United States is fighting a land war of steadily growing proportions in Asia."[6]

Biographer Doris Kearns Goodwin wrote in *Lyndon Johnson and the American Dream* that in July, 1965, Defense Secretary McNamara "presented the president with three options: to cut our losses and withdraw, to continue fighting at the current level, or to substantially expand our military pressure."[7] Expanded pressure for U.S. Army Chief of Staff General William Westmoreland meant increasing troop levels from 82,000 to 175,000, a force that would allow Westmoreland to take the "war to the enemy."

Standing before the group of electric co-op leaders, Johnson mentioned none of the specific recommendations of his military advisers, but he acknowledged the special role co-ops played in the international effort. His speech was typed on small cream-colored note cards, but Johnson ad-libbed on the subject that seemed to dominate his every thought:

> There are three billion people in this world and America has less than two hundred million of them. So for every American you find there are fifteen others. And there is hardly a corner of this big earth, where three billion people live, where rural electrification is not needed now as much as it was needed when Roosevelt came to this town and issued an Executive Order creating the REA.[8]

There was one specific corner of the earth Johnson wanted electrified. In 1965, approximately eleven million of South Vietnam's fourteen million people did not have central station electricity, and less than one hundred of the country's three thousand villages had any type of electric power. Electrifying these villages, Johnson believed, could turn the tide in South Vietnam, changing their way of life forever. It could even help win the war.

Robert Komer, best known as LBJ's point man "to win the hearts and minds in Vietnam," said Johnson, "saw the Vietnamese farmer as being like the Texas farmer . . .We're going to provide them with rural electricity . . ."[9]

LBJ saw the parallels of his own personal story in the Texas Hill Country, having lived on a farm with no electricity, watching his mother bent on her knees scrubbing clothes in a washtub. One farm wife who had moved from town to the Hill Country said it "was like moving from the twentieth century back into the Middle Ages."[10] It also appeared the Hill Country would be the last place in America to get power lines.

The REA had repeatedly denied requests for loans, arguing the people of the Hill Country were too poor and couldn't pay their bills. The area also failed to meet the REA's criteria for density: The agency would not make a loan in which electric lines would serve an average of less than three farms per mile. When a group of co-op leaders from five counties approached the REA about a loan for a new Pedernales Electric Cooperative, they were told, "You have too much land and not enough people."

The Texas Hill Country, however, had voted in a dynamo of a freshman congressman. LBJ visited court houses, school houses, and barbecues, telling his constituents he would get them electricity if they signed up for their local co-op. "I'll go to the REA," he said. "I'll go to the president if I have to."[11] First, though, he had to address their fear of the wires killing their cattle, or losing their land if they signed a paper joining an electric co-op. They had to pay five dollars to join Pedernales Electric Co-op, and few people had five dollars to spare. LBJ used his vast powers of persuasion, telling the farm wives they would "look younger at forty than your mother" because of the conveniences of electricity.

Then he did what he said he'd do, meeting with REA administrator Carmody and requesting a waiver of the density rules. Carmody refused. Johnson took the request to a higher level, securing a meeting with FDR.

LBJ himself told different stories about how be lobbied the president to waive the density requirement on two separate occasions. At the first meeting, FDR rebuffed him. At the second, Johnson would not be denied. The president called Carmody to tell him the density requirements would not be an issue. "I'll gamble on these folks," FDR said. "They breed pretty fast down there."

A telegram arrived at the Pedernales Electric Co-op office informing them that the REA had approved the loan. Soon, the lines went up and the lights started to flicker. Nevertheless, many believed that farm families would not pay their bills. Johnson told "the scoffers" that he would wager a Stetson hat for every family in his district that did not pay for electricity.

"I never lost a single hat," he said. And soon something else happened, too. A legend was born as parents all over the Texas Hill Country were soon naming their babies after Lyndon Johnson. Pulitzer Prize-winning biographer Robert Caro believes that something happened to LBJ as he brought his constituents electricity: He realized his genius to use the power of government "to help people who are fighting forces too big for themselves."

He had done all of this as a lowly, back-bencher congressman. Now, as president, what could stop him from bringing rural electrification to South Vietnam? He had vast resources at his disposal, including the experts with him in the Rose Garden.

The president told the electric co-op leaders, "I am very grateful to all of you, and to Clyde Ellis, for the fine support that you are giving to our efforts to try and provide leadership, economic assistance, and rural electrification to Southeast Asia." LBJ had read Ellis's letter about Vietnam with interest, personally directing White House staffers Bill Moyers and Richard Goodwin to take action. Soon thereafter, Congress approved $5 million for the creation of electric co-ops in South Vietnam.[12]

That year, NRECA organized two Vietnamese electric co-ops, and caught the attention of *Newsweek* columnist Kenneth Crawford. "These experts see no reason why the know-how they have accumulated in the last thirty years, while bringing electricity to 98 percent of American farms . . . can't succeed in relatively secure parts of South Vietnam."[13] Johnson saw rural electrification in Vietnam in far starker terms: "This is the only way that I know in which we can really win the battle against communism."[14]

Yet, in his Rose Garden speech, Johnson knew the conflict would be less about diesel generators and more about young boys on patrols and bombs dropped from B-52s. To win the war, he needed the American people to show resolve.

"Where we have commitments, we intend to keep them," LBJ told the gathering, again deviating from the note cards.[15]

> Now, there are going to be long debates, there are going to be some eloquent speeches, there are going to be differences of opinion, and there is going to be criticism of your president. But three presidents—President Eisenhower, President Kennedy, and your present president—have made a commitment in the name of the people of the United States, and our national honor is at stake in Southeast Asia . . .

Johnson also had a prediction. "Now there are going to be some dark days and there are going to be some times when we call on you for some help, and I don't think you will be found wanting."

After his talk, LBJ, as his daily diary noted, "milled around in the Garden" talking to co-op directors.[16] The electric co-op delegation departed the White House, traveling to a hotel to see a movie about a new electric co-op in Ecuador. Soon thereafter, the full text of Johnson's speech was released to the press corps. Years later, this speech would give historians a window into LBJ's decision-making about Vietnam. For some, the speech in front of electric co-op leaders contained a startling revelation.

LBJ had, for the first time, announced the escalation of the war in Vietnam.

Historian Brian VanDeMark, author of *Into the Quagmire: Lyndon Johnson and the Escalation of the Vietnam War*, concluded that "the clearest, most unmistakable clue to Johnson's intention came during a Rose Garden speech to the National Rural Electric Cooperative Association . . . Having privately debated and personally struggled over Vietnam for weeks, LBJ appeared resigned to a larger war."[17]

Another historian believes LBJ showed remarkable clarity about his dark road ahead. Biographer Robert Dallek recounts in his book *Flawed Giant*, "At a Rose Garden gathering of rural electric cooperative officials on the fourteenth, the president predicted that long debates and criticism of him were in the offing over Vietnam."[18]

At a press conference two weeks later, the American people learned what electric co-op leaders had been told privately in the Rose Garden. The president was expanding the war in Vietnam.

Perhaps electric co-op leaders did not understand the gravity of what they had been told, but they kept their commitment. In 1965, Ellis admitted he did not "know what course the war in South

Vietnam will eventually take, or what the outcome of our efforts will be."[19]

He would soon learn the challenges. Robert Komer recalled a time when he discovered two rural electrification engineers in a South Vietnam province, installing poles and a diesel generator.[20] They told him they could wire a village in about four months, leading Komer to conclude, "It will be in the year 3000 before we have rural electrification in Vietnam." Komer once jokingly told LBJ, "Boss, why don't we win the war first. Then we'll turn on the lights."[21] Johnson was not amused.

"Unless you can guard what you're doing, you can't do anything," LBJ told U.S. Senator Mike Mansfield. "We can't build an airport, by God, much less an REA line . . . That's why we had to limit it to just three or four REA projects and one little dam."[22]

On September 23, 1965, Ellis would suffer a serious heart attack. His frenetic pace—his travels to South Vietnam and meetings across America to give one-hundred-minute speeches—had caught up with him. He was forced to take a leave of absence, but in 1966, he published a critically acclaimed autobiography on his history with rural electrification titled *A Giant Step*.

Meanwhile, LBJ passed landmark legislation at an amazing clip: Medicare, the Housing Act, and the Voting Rights Act. But he never stopped defending electric co-ops. In 1966, U.S. Senator Richard Russell of Georgia complained to LBJ during a phone call that the 2 percent interest rate on REA loans was too low, claiming incredulously that "co-ops are paying their managers $27,500 a year." Johnson stood his ground.[23] "Only the poor get the lower rate," he said.

For all his Great Society success, there was always Vietnam. What LBJ told electric co-op leaders in the Rose Garden in 1965 turned out to be true, the criticism, the dark days, and the realization that his decision to send large numbers of ground troops would result in the end of his presidency. In 1965, Johnson's popularity rating was 70 percent; by 1967, it was down to 39 percent.

Both LBJ and Ellis would both realize that America was embroiled in a conflict that could not be won by stringing wire and electrifying villages. South Vietnam was not the Hill Country of Texas. There was no mail service in most of the hamlets across Vietnam for people to pay their bills. The Viet Cong would often cut the co-op power lines. There were exploding mortars, massive air strikes, and machine gun fire, issues that the Hill Country never had to contend with. "Viet Cong activity is increasing in all Project Areas," a 1967 NRECA-USAID report noted. Electric co-op leaders had transformed rural America, but they were powerless to win the Vietnam War.

———— • ◆ • ————

LBJ decided not to seek reelection in 1968, but he again sought out his old friends to tell his side of the story. Vaughn Davis Bornet in his book, *The Presidency of Lyndon Johnson*, wrote, "Perhaps every presidential administration has a verbal 'last hurrah.' For Lyndon Johnson that came on the occasion of a speech . . . to the [National] Rural Electric Cooperative Association."[24]

It was February 27, 1968. Traveling in an unmarked car at the head of an informal motorcade of media and Secret Service agents, Johnson made a historic first visit to Dallas since Kennedy's assassination.[25] The trip was masked in secrecy; reporters were not informed of his plans until his plane left from Austin. Only then were they told the destination was Dallas's Memorial Auditorium, where eight thousand electric co-op leaders had gathered for the NRECA Annual Meeting. Along the route to the auditorium,

Johnson passed within sight of the location where Kennedy was shot. He appeared to take no notice.

With tight security and in the shadow of a giant Willie Wiredhand poster, LBJ gave a forceful speech reminiscing about his days forming Pedernales Electric Co-op. "Your vision has helped tipped the balance before when the REA rescued the countryside from depression and darkness," he said. "Rural America 1968 shines with the blessings you have brought it for thirty years."[26] As always, he said all the right things, touching on the urban-rural divide, and the importance of fresh sources of capital for future electric co-op growth. But he could not escape the specter of the Vietnam War, and he didn't try.

"There will be blood, sweat, and tears ahead," he shouted. "The weak will drop from the lines, their feet sore, and their voices loud." Even his strongest electric co-op supporters had grown weary of the war. *The New York Times* noted Johnson "drew warmer applause for his pledge to continue assisting rural electrification than for his firmly delivered statement on Vietnam."[27]

If Vietnam continued to haunt him, he clung to the issue for which no one could dispute his leadership. In the twilight of his presidency, LBJ could be found at his ranch playing with his grandson and talking to guests about his fight to bring rural electrification to the Hill Country. Getting the recognition he deserved turned out to be a different story.[28]

Year after year, other leaders of the rural electric program received NRECA's Distinguished Service Award, the highest honor bestowed on an elected official. LBJ was passed over, or worse, forgotten. "He was a short-changed because of the Vietnam War," said Glenn English. "He should have received it while he was in office."[29] English decided to do something about it: He made an executive decision to posthumously present LBJ the award.

In 2002, the 60th NRECA Annual Meeting again returned to Dallas. Luci Johnson, standing in for her eighty-nine-year old mother, Lady Bird, accepted the award for her late father. "Frankly, I'd be scared the heavens might have really lit up with Daddy's disappointment if I hadn't come," she said. She read a letter from Lady Bird in which she recalled LBJ standing with an elderly woman who was reaching up to turn on the light for the first time in her farm home. Lady Bird wrote that such moments "gave him more satisfaction than almost anything he accomplished over his years of public service."

The accolades, long overdue, kept coming. In 2011, Pedernales Electric Co-op unveiled an Official Texas Historical Marker honoring LBJ's tireless dedication to the Hill Country. Mike Williams, CEO of the Texas Electric Cooperatives, said: "LBJ was like a force of nature. He knew what it was like to live without the quality of life that electricity eventually brought to rural America. He was determined to bring light to farms, ranches, and small towns all across this country."[30]

In the final years of his life, LBJ, the president who could have become an REA administrator, wrote John Carmody, the man he would have replaced: "Of all of the things I have ever done, nothing has given me as much satisfaction as bringing power to the Hill Country of Texas. Today in my home county, we have full grown men who have never seen a kerosene lamp except possibly in a movie—and that is all to the good."[31]

———— • ✦ • ————

By 1968, America's electric co-ops were serving nearly five million consumer members across a vastly changing landscape. More Americans now lived in the suburbs than in the cities, and the growth into once rural areas required new sources of capital. With worries over the future availability of REA loan funds, electric co-ops would soon begin the National Rural Utilities Cooperative Finance Corporation (CFC).

In 1968, Clyde Ellis retired as NRECA general manager after building an infant trade association into a national lobbying power-house. Robert (Bob) Partridge was officially named his successor at the 1968 NRECA Annual Meeting.

A Missouri-native, Partridge started his career at the REA after a three-year tour of duty in the South Pacific during World War II. By 1973, he was America's highest-ranking reserve officer, holding the rank of Major General. Arriving at NRECA in 1961, he served as a legislative representative. After Ellis suffered his heart attack, Partridge also served as acting general manager.

Though blessed with a powerful baritone voice, he could not rival Ellis as an orator. However, he possessed an unrivaled knowl-edge of NRECA's membership. Mattie Olson, a longtime NRECA executive, claimed that Partridge knew the name of every electric co-op general manager and board president in the country. He also knew the electric utility business. Wallace Tillman, an NRECA lobbyist who later headed the association's Energy Policy division, remarked, "Bob Partridge knew everything about generation."[32]

He would need all these skills to face the incoming Nixon administration. Richard Nixon, who had resurrected his political career after losing a California gubernatorial race in 1962, had narrowly defeated Vice President Hubert Humphrey in the 1968 presidential contest.

Nixon's campaign was cagey, sending a taped message to an NRECA regional meeting in which the candidate said, "I favor the continuation of a favorable interest rate situation" for REA.[33] Partridge waited to see if Nixon was true to his words or if he would return to the anti-REA policies of the Eisenhower era. During the 1972 Christmas holiday, the question was definitively answered.

On December 29, 1972, President Nixon was at Camp David and Harry Truman had just been buried in the presidential library courtyard in Independence, Missouri. It was also the day the U.S. Department of Agriculture announced via a 4 p.m. press release that it was wiping out REA's 2 percent direct loan program. U.S. Agriculture Secretary Earl Butz and REA administrator David Hamil could not initially explain any details. NRECA would learn that future electric co-op loans would be made under the new Rural Development Act and would disqualify all but ninety of the nearly one thousand electric co-ops.

"When I got the telephone message that Friday afternoon, I felt as if April Fools' Day had come three months early," Partridge said.[34] But it was not April Fools' Day. It was to become infamously known in the electric co-op program as *Black Friday*.

Partridge now faced the challenge of a lifetime. He announced he would urge "President Nixon to reconsider the decision and would solicit support in Congress to put pressure on the White House."

For the next few months, Partridge brought the pressure. Nixon found himself dogged not only by two enterprising reporters from *The Washington Post* named Bob Woodward and Carl Bernstein, but also by electric co-ops intent on salvaging the REA—and their reputation.

In January 1973, as Nixon officials plotted against electric co-ops in the
White House, electric co-op leaders were nearly blowing the roof off
of the Mayflower Hotel in Washington, D.C.

6

THE ELECTRIC
CO-OP TAPES

O N JANUARY 31, 1973, PRESIDENT RICHARD M. NIXON
held a televised press conference, just one day after former
White House aides G. Gordon Liddy and James McCord, Jr.
were convicted of conspiracy, burglary, and wiretapping of the
Democratic National Committee's Watergate Headquarters in
Washington, D.C. The White House press corps was starved for
news. It had been 112 days since the president's last news conference, and there were many issues to cover: The Vietnam War still
roiled, and the Watergate convictions had led *The New York Times* to
editorialize, "This proves that this sinister operation was no trivial
escapade by unimportant persons."[1]

President Nixon was ready, too. Entering the hot, claustrophobic
briefing room, he was prepared, in his own words, to take "off the
gloves" and let the press corps know he'd "no longer uncomplain-
ingly accept their barbs or allow their unaccountable power go
unchallenged."[2] Nixon was emboldened. Only three months before,
he'd won a stunning electoral victory over Democratic U.S. Senator
George McGovern, including 68 percent of the rural vote. It was a

mandate, Nixon believed, to cut a government that he deemed "too big and expensive."

The day after the election, Nixon told the White House staff, "There are no sacred cows."[3] His budget, released only days before the press conference, repudiated FDR's New Deal and LBJ's Great Society. His administration was also inviting a constitutional showdown by impounding money already appropriated by the U.S. Congress. And as Richard Nixon took the podium in the White House briefing room, he would not mince any words.

The early questions from the press corps were all too predictable. Nixon easily fielded inquires on Vietnam, prisoners of war, and amnesty for draft resisters. Curiously, the word *Watergate* was absent. *The New York Times* reported, "From a distance of fifteen feet, Nixon showed no nervousness. He did not hesitate. He was not tongue-tied. Indeed, he was so voluble that his replies seemed longer than before."[4]

Six questions into the press conference, the president appeared untouchable. He then called upon a flame-haired reporter named Sarah McClendon who was skilled at baiting the president.

"Mr. President, sir," McClendon said. "Senator Hollings said on a recent trip to Southeast Asia, he discovered that we are letting some countries, including Japan, have 2 percent money, yet we have denied our own farmers in rural cooperatives 2 percent money. We are telling them they have to have their loans at 5 percent. Would you comment on this . . .?"[5]

President Nixon knew the issue well. Only days before, he had boasted to a group of Republican leaders about overhauling the REA. But he still seemed annoyed, as if the electric co-ops had encroached upon the narrative of his press conference.

The president responded, "Let me say, if I could, with regard to REA—and Miss McClendon, because you are somewhat of an expert on this—I have always supported REA because I used to represent the old 12th District." Nixon had won his congressional seat in Southern California by defeating U.S. Representative Jerry Voorhis, a diehard New Dealer and later the head of the Cooperative League of the USA. For NRECA, Nixon was no Jerry Voorhis, and NRECA had the voting records to back it up.

"When I lived there and represented it," Nixon continued, "it was primarily agricultural, orange groves; now it is primarily people, subdivided. But as one who came from that area, I naturally had a great interest in this matter of the REA and supported it."

McClendon believed Nixon respected her concern for rural issues. After complaining to Nixon about a drought in Texas, the president had sent her on a plane to view the devastation.[6] This time, however, Nixon had taken the bait.

"But what I have found is that when I first voted for REA," Nixon said, "80 percent of the loans went for the purpose of rural development and getting electricity to farms. Now, 80 percent of this 2 percent money goes for country clubs and dilettantes, for example, and others who can afford living in the country. I am not for 2 percent money for people who can afford 5 percent or 7."[7]

Country clubs and dilettantes. Decades later, these four words still cause electric co-op leaders to shudder. Electric co-ops were accustomed to being attacked. The big power companies and editorial writers had been doing it for decades, but never before had a U.S. president unleashed such incendiary rhetoric in a public forum. Nixon had created a caricature of rural America as a place of wealth and leisure, of retired corporate executives and spoiled rich girls. It was a rural America that electric co-op leaders did not recognize.

Nixon was not finished with his assault. Questioned about whether the administration's action to impound funds was constitutional, Nixon replied, "Now the point is, the Congress has to decide, does it want to raise taxes in order to spend more or does it want to cut, as the president wants to cut." He jabbed at special interests. "The Interior Committee wants to have more parks and the Agriculture Committee wants cheap REA loans . . ."

When the press conference ended, Nixon was ebullient. Gloating to White House Press Secretary Ron Ziegler, Nixon said he "drove them right up the wall" on the impoundment issue.[8] The REA question was another matter. Speaking with his loyal presidential assistant, Pat Buchanan, Nixon said, "Sarah had her usual mountain of—" before Buchanan interrupted a likely expletive.[9] Then the two men discussed the subject that would not go away.

"I was stunned there was no Watergate thing even mentioned," Buchanan said. Nixon believed the press had simply run out of time and the questions about Watergate would persist. They plotted the White House response to the inevitable press inquiries about whether they supported Senator Sam Ervin's Watergate Committee.

"I don't approve of espionage," Nixon told Buchanan. Nixon's press conference was a success, marred perhaps only by the "usual mountain of—" from Sarah McClendon. It was also a day that the issue of REA had trumped the Watergate scandal. It would not be the last.

The next day, February 1, 1973, President Nixon's hyperbole at his press conference put Agriculture Secretary Butz in the hot seat as he testified before the U.S. Senate Agriculture Committee, the equivalent of home-field advantage for electric co-ops. Butz came under withering scrutiny for the president's claims of past support for REA and his unsubstantiated assertion about *country clubs and dilettantes.*"

Using statistics provided by NRECA, Senator McGovern pointed out that Nixon had voted thirteen out of sixteen times against electric co-op positions while in Congress. Senator

Humphrey also grilled Butz about Nixon's assertions that electric co-ops served the wealthiest Americans.

"One-tenth of 1 percent are country clubs," said Humphrey. "That's purer than Ivory Snow, Mr. Secretary."[10] As television lights glared in his face, Butz struggled to respond, calling the president's choice of words "unfortunate and probably not premeditated."

Butz was in a corner, dissembling. The White House taping system revealed much about the Nixon administration—many believe the recordings ultimately forced Nixon to resign. These tapes also told a different story than what Butz testified to the committee, revealing a White House struggling to respond to the intransigence of electric co-ops.

On January 24, 1973, just days before Nixon's press conference, the president's cabinet convened in the White House. Sitting in comfortable leather chairs around an oval mahogany table, Nixon listened as Butz labeled the REA loan program "ridiculous" and claimed the government was "financing electricity for retired corporate executives who have a nice home in the country."[11]

Coffee cups can be heard ringing off the fine china as the Cabinet members discussed a possible compromise. Butz called electric co-ops "powerful, politically powerful." If they cut a deal with NRECA and Congress, Butz believed, the administration "may not lose the whole thing." U.S. Treasury Secretary George Shultz wasn't so sure he wanted to concede an inch.

"Where can we hold the line?" Shultz demanded, if they couldn't cut a 2 percent loan program for "retired corporate executives." President Nixon remained silent during the REA debate, but he harbored a strong opinion. Two days later, on January 26, 1973, the topic came up again. Nixon finally spoke his mind.

This time, a group of Republican leaders convened in the Cabinet Room, including Vice President Spiro Agnew, U.S.

Representative Gerald Ford, and George H.W. Bush, chairman of
the Republican National Committee. The topic of the REA sur-
faced three times during the meeting, led by White House Office
of Management and Budget (OMB) Director Caspar Weinberger.
Nicknamed "Cap the Knife" for his ruthless cost-cutting ability,
Weinberger argued there was no economic justification for 2 percent
loans for 80 percent nonfarm uses, which he described as "suburban
developments, country clubs, and recreational developments."[12]

Then Nixon interjected, and the Cabinet Room became eerily
quiet. "All of the members know, as I know from long experience,"
Nixon warned, "the electric co-ops are one of the most vicious lob-
bies you'll ever run up against."

———— • ◆ • ————

The acrimony of NRECA's battles during the Eisenhower administration, which Nixon experienced firsthand as vice president, had
again reared its head. Nixon said the right thing about the REA
when it was politically expedient; his true animus toward electric
co-ops was unleashed after he had won a second term, and was
politically untouchable.

As Nixon officials plotted behind closed doors in the White
House, electric co-op leaders were nearly blowing the roof off one
of the most storied hotels in Washington, D.C., at a time when
LBJ, one of their greatest champions, had passed away at his ranch
in Texas.

On January 23 and 24, fourteen hundred rural leaders packed
into the Mayflower Hotel for arguably the most famous legislative
gathering in NRECA history. It was part strategy session, part pep
rally, and 100 percent "electric" according to NRECA's Mattie Olson.
A giant banner that read *We Protest* hung from the ballroom

balcony. Angus Hastings, a longtime Florida electric co-op leader, was among those wearing *"Save Rural Electrification"* stickers.

"We were really into it," Hastings recollects. "There were a lot of upset people. This was one time we had unity."[13] Senator Humphrey had a raging fever, but his speech at the Mayflower is considered one of the finest ever delivered to an electric co-op audience.

"You can use what has been done to demonstrate whether or not one man, by executive order, can ignore the will of the American people through the Congress assembled," Humphrey shouted. "You can determine once and for all whether or not a president can continue to impound funds that have been appropriated by Congress."

Electric co-op leaders descended upon Capitol Hill and lobbied for legislation to save the REA program. Some carried kerosene lanterns. Howard Crinklaw, a legendary electric co-op manager at Douglas Electric in Roseburg, Oregon, had his REA loan wiped out because of Nixon's action. Douglas Electric served struggling timber communities that could ill-afford a rate increase. Crinklaw met with Republican U.S. Representative John Dellenback, who said he would not help until he "studied the issue." Crinklaw couldn't wait. "We flooded the sucker with letters," he said.[14] Dellenback soon called Crinklaw. "Call off your people. I got the message."

Stories like this were occurring all over Capitol Hill, and the White House was on the defensive. Congressional Democrats were already in no mood to work with Nixon, and Republicans were already feeling the brunt of the president's attack on rural programs. "The White House doesn't know an ear of corn from a bale of hay," said one Republican congressman.[15]

Methodically, NRECA worked on Capitol Hill to override Nixon's action. On February 21, the U.S. Senate approved a bill to require the president to reinstate the REA loan program. Humphrey built his case on constitutional grounds. "The loan-making authority of the Rural Electrification Act of 1936 was created by Congress to carry out a policy to be declared in the public interest," Humphrey said on the Senate floor. "The Act did not say to the Executive Branch, 'Carry out this policy if you like it.'"[16]

Nixon had another problem. On March 21, 1973, White House counsel John Dean told President Nixon, "We have a cancer—within—close to the presidency that's growing."[17] He told the president that the Watergate burglars were demanding money. They would need one million dollars to end the blackmail. "We could get that . . ." the president replied. "And you could get it in cash."

On April 4, 1973, the U.S. House of Representatives also overwhelmingly passed legislation to update the REA loan program. In early May, more than seven hundred electric co-op leaders returned to Washington, D.C., to watch the U.S. Congress finish the job and send REA legislation (S. 394) to the White House with a veto-proof margin. The NRECA May Legislative Conference was so successful it continues to this day, with nearly three thousand electric co-op leaders making the pilgrimage annually. The updated REA program called for 5 percent loans, but included 2 percent loans for those systems in "hardship" areas.

The REA legislation reached the president's desk at a time when Nixon realized he could be impeached. On May 11, the day the president was scheduled to sign S. 394, the web of deceit had expanded to questions about the use of the CIA in the cover-up, and wiretapping of the press corps and National Security Council. That afternoon, Nixon met with White House Chief of Staff Alexander Haig in the Executive Office Building adjacent to the White House. Nixon fought to defend his position. "[I am] the one person that's totally blameless in this," he told Haig.[18]

An hour later, Nixon, Butz, and David Hamil met for the signing ceremony. The president's White House statement noted,

"Thirty-eight years ago today, President Franklin Roosevelt signed Executive Order 7037 to create the Rural Electrification Administration. On this anniversary date, I am pleased to sign into law S. 394, a bill making significant improvements in the REA program."[19]

The bill signing ceremony took six minutes. No electric co-op leaders had been invited, but the ceremonial pens distributed at such events seemed trivial compared to the larger picture. For 131 days, NRECA and its members had kept the pressure on Congress to overturn Nixon's elimination of the REA program. Electric co-ops had survived the most vicious attack against their program since its inception. Partridge called the legislation a "victory for the people who stood solidly against the capitulation to the administration's edict of December 29."[20] The REA was alive, but Richard Nixon's fate still hung in the balance.

Soon, the Senate Watergate Committee would begin televised hearings. They revealed lies and hush money, a conspiracy to conceal the roles of top Nixon officials, and a campaign of political espionage and political sabotage. In the face of growing impeachment, Richard Nixon resigned on August 8, 1974.

For five strange months in 1973, the darkest period in the rural electric program and the darkest period in the history of the presidency ran in bizarre tandem. NRECA's Black Friday became a microcosm of the larger and more insidious Watergate scandal. While Nixon's sneak attack on REA had failed, Partridge realized how close his membership had been to defeat. "This demonstrates that [we] have molded ourselves into a force that won't let the electric co-op program die in politics," he declared.

The political "force" that Partridge spoke of was at the zenith of its powers. They were organized and unified, shielded by a bipartisan group of powerful, aging leaders in the Congress, many of whom remembered when the lights came on. But these lawmakers would not be around forever. There were other warning signs, too.

The primary allegations of their opponents: that electric co-ops were now serving more suburban, affluent areas; that the country was now electrified and no longer required a deep subsidy, only began to intensify. Concern about the federal deficit lingered and a permanent group of bureaucrats opposed to the REA were in key government positions at the Office of Management and Budget. It would not be long before electric co-ops would feel the true power of this obscure agency.

———— • ◆ • ————

In 1974, a new generation of rural leaders emerged in the U.S. Congress. Bob Bergland, a Minnesota congressman with one of the nation's highest farm populations, was described by political analysts as a "good example of how a politically astute congressman can turn a marginal seat into a safe one." Bergland climbed the ladder on the House Agriculture Committee where he was a vocal critic of Nixon's agriculture policies.

Glenn English, the state director of the Oklahoma Democratic Party, waged a vigorous campaign in the state's 6th District, prevailing in one of the election year's biggest upsets. English won by a solid margin and carried solid Republican counties. *Congressional Quarterly* concluded, "Judging from the acumen that won the race for him," English should be a solid favorite in future races. He also received a coveted slot on the House Agriculture Committee.

The new president was Gerald R. Ford, a gregarious pipe-smoking former congressman from Michigan. His record of voting with electric co-ops was marginal at best. From 1949 to 1973, Ford cast seventy-one votes on rural electrification issues. Only eleven times did he support NRECA's position. But he had something else going for him: He was not Richard Nixon. The prognosis for Gerald Ford, according to electric co-op leaders, was "one of waiting and seeing—with a dash of mild hope."[21]

Ford had also been critical of the Tennessee Valley Authority, a key supplier of electricity for public power in the South. TVA became a surprise, and some say defining issue in Ford's primary election against former California Governor Ronald Reagan. In the tumultuous world that is presidential politics, a federal corporation Ford had criticized in the U.S. House would help save his future as America's president.

NRECA General Manager Bob Partridge led the effort to block the Nixon administration's attempt to eliminate the REA.

President Gerald R. Ford greets Youth Tour participants in the White House in 1976.
That day in the White House, President Ford was also dealing with
the assassination of a U.S. Ambassador.

7

ONE DAY IN
THE VALLEY

President Ford was in deep political trouble. On May 25, 1976, as six states were holding Republican primaries, he prepared to lose five of the contests to Ronald Reagan. "I had no illusions about Arkansas, Nevada, Idaho, Kentucky, and Tennessee," Ford recounted. "Reagan was just too strong."[1]

The two men were locked in mortal combat for delegates and Reagan had surged ahead 528 to 479. Incredibly, with all the advantages of the presidency, Ford was now an underdog to win the nomination of his own political party. Winning the primary in his home state of Michigan had given him a slight boost, but the momentum would evaporate if he was routed on May 25. Ford dreaded what was to come. "The psychological impact of expected defeat," he noted, "can just be as damaging as defeat itself."

Venerable *Washington Post* reporter David Broder assessed the situation in his column. "How did a palpably honest president, who has brought his party back from its worst disgrace, find himself trailing in the race for the nomination?" Broder answered his own question. "It is the inability of Mr. Ford to define the goals, the vision, and the purposes of his presidency in a way that gives coherence to his administration and to his campaign."[2]

Ford needed to limit the damage, but he did not expect help from conservative Tennessee or Kentucky, two of the bigger delegate hauls of the night. This was Reagan country. *The Tennessean* newspaper concluded, "A Reagan victory in Tennessee, of course, could be another nail in an already closing coffin for Ford."[3] His supporters were even hedging their bets. Republican U.S. Senator Howard Baker of Tennessee, chairman of Ford's campaign, invited Reagan to spend the night at his home.

Days before the May 25 primary, Reagan came to Knoxville, Tennessee, to help put the final nail in the coffin. During a routine television interview, he was asked if he would consider dismantling TVA and turning it over to a private enterprise. It was a question any candidate in the region needed to be prepared to answer. While not without its detractors, TVA is interwoven into the fabric of the Tennessee Valley. It is an important supplier of electricity to electric co-ops and municipal utilities, and it employs a vast number of people. As a General Electric spokesman in the 1950s and '60s, Reagan himself had been chastised by a GE executive for attacking TVA in his speeches.[4] GE sold turbines to TVA, and it was bad for business.

In 1964, GOP Republican nominee Barry Goldwater had been lambasted for claiming TVA should be dismantled. Reagan, having participated in that campaign, was well aware of the dangerous vortex of TVA politics. He knew the potential fallout, but Reagan said what he believed. Privatizing TVA, Reagan answered, "would be something to look at."[5]

Reagan's aides flinched when they heard his answer. And President Ford's team pounced, accusing Reagan of supporting higher electric rates and a loss of jobs. Sensing opportunity, Ford sought out a group of reporters at the White House. "I fully support TVA," he said. In an instant, the trajectory of the Republican primary had been spun off its axis.

David Callis, general manager of the Tennessee Electric Cooperative Association, said, "TVA may have issues to deal with, but they're family and we'll deal with them internally. And may God have mercy on the occasional congressman from New York that dares to attack it."[6]

In this case, it was a presidential candidate, and as word of Reagan's "attack" on TVA echoed throughout the South, Ford's high command sensed a momentum shift. A confidential campaign memo outlined how "Reagan's statements on TVA" had buoyed the president's support in Kentucky and Tennessee.[7] The President Ford Committee was "working hard to capitalize on last week's developments." Even Senator Baker was castigating his houseguest. Ford Communications Director Dave Gergen argued that the TVA issue would allow the Democrats to paint Reagan as an extremist. "No one who has ever been successfully branded as an extremist has ever won the presidency."

On the day of the primary, President Ford was campaigning in California. He had no chance to defeat Reagan there, but he was forcing him to fight for his home state. Ford awaited election results from his room at the Holiday Inn, hopeful that things would break his way in the South. It was a roller coaster of a night, particularly in Tennessee. President Ford took an early lead, then later in the night, fell far behind. He rallied again, only to see his lead whittled to 123 votes. When it was over, nearly two hundred fifty thousand ballots were cast in Tennessee. Ford had edged Reagan by 2,170 votes. "The TVA issue turned things around for me in Tennessee," the president wrote. "It probably helped me in Kentucky, where I won an upset victory."[8]

The Ford campaign had new life. "When you're supposed to be beaten in five races out of six, and you lose only three, the press interprets that as a victory," Ford wrote. *Washington Post* columnists Roland Evans and Robert Novak suggested that Reagan's "TVA gaffe could be more damaging to him in the long run than in the short run."[9]

It also may have ended Reagan's chances at the nomination. Ford press aide, Peter Kaye, said, "Michigan stopped Reagan, and Tennessee and Kentucky turned it around. Then all we had to do was play out the string."[10]

By pummeling Reagan into submission on TVA, the president appeared to be the second coming of George Norris, the father of TVA. He wasn't. Raymond Kuhl, who headed the Michigan Electric Cooperative Association for seventeen years, said that Republican congressmen in Michigan were greatly influenced by the major state power companies, Consumers Power Company and Detroit Edison.[11] Perhaps this explains why after voting against a bill to expand TVA in 1959, Ford wrote his constituents that "TVA has now come to maturity. It is time to cut it loose from mother's apron strings."[12]

TVA is governed by a board of directors and after the May primary, Ford nominated Thomas L. Longshore, an official with the Alabama Power Company, often a foe of TVA in the South. Partridge believed the appointment showed a "callous disregard for the views of rural electric and public power leaders of the TVA area."[13]

Partridge met with White House officials and urged that "someone more in tune philosophically with the purposes and objectives of TVA be named." The White House ignored Partridge's concerns, although he eventually heard from the Federal Bureau of Investigation, questioning his opposition to the nominee. Ford's support for TVA, it appeared, had its limitations.

———◆———

While Ford and Reagan battled for delegates throughout the summer, on June 16, 1976, the president faced an unexpected international crisis. And a group of emerging electric co-op leaders from the Rural Electric Youth Tour would gain an insider's view of history afforded to few Americans. To this day, few students most likely appreciate the significance of what they experienced at the White House.

Just after noon that day, Ford convened his national security advisers.[14] The group included Vice President Nelson Rockefeller, Secretary of State Henry Kissinger, CIA Director George H.W. Bush, and Ford's Chief of Staff, Dick Cheney. Earlier, the president had learned that U.S. Ambassador to Lebanon Francis E. Meloy and Counselor for Economic Affairs Robert O. Waring had been abducted in Lebanon on their way to visit the new president-elect of the country. The waiting game was on, but Ford's national security team expected the men to be released safely.

It was another frenetic day in the White House. President Ford had twenty scheduled appointments, including nine hundred high school students in the East Room as part of NRECA's "Government in Action Youth Tour."[15] The Youth Tour tradition inspired by LBJ had thrived. Ford intended to keep his commitment, but he was now consumed with the news from the Middle East.

As the national security meeting began, CIA Director Bush revealed that unidentified bodies had been found on a beach near Beirut.[16] Shortly after 1 p.m., Secretary of State Kissinger was handed a manila envelope that confirmed their worst fears: Meloy and Waring had been assassinated. For nearly an hour, the national security team went into crisis mode, reviewing their options, including a possible evacuation of the fourteen hundred Americans living in Lebanon.

Meanwhile, the Youth Tour students assembled in the East Room. The young men were wearing loud prints and wide ties, and the women were in their finest dresses, as they jockeyed for position. A White House memo recommended that the East Room piano be removed lest the students stand on it to see the president.[17]

Soon, a grim-faced Ford read a statement to the press corps about the assassination. "They were on a mission of peace, seeking to do what they could in the service of their country to help restore order, stability, and reason to Lebanon."[18] There was little time to contemplate the unfolding crisis. Ford returned to the Oval Office and for two minutes conferred with Dick Cheney. Then at 4:18 p.m., the president entered the East Room. There he found awestruck Youth Tour students completely unaware of the gravity of the moment.

Ford told the students, "For four decades, electric cooperatives have brought power to rural areas." Reading from remarks written in giant capital letters, he added, "Perhaps no group better understands the essentials of conservation and planning in energy use than this one."[19] Polaroid cameras flashed in President Ford's face as he discussed incentives for alternative forms of energy such as solar, geothermal, and wind power.

Ford said nothing about the situation in Lebanon. He graciously accepted a Willie Wiredhand statue and a dozen NRECA-logo golf balls from NRECA President John Dolinger of Tennessee. Ford also met with the newly elected board of the Youth Consulting Council, including its new president, Matt Rhoades of Illinois. Rhoades was seventeen and unaware of the tragedy that had unfolded that day. Rhoades said Ford "seemed very somber, a bit rushed. But he was very polite and courteous."[20] The students, only feet away, had no idea that they were in closer proximity to a president than most people in their lifetime.

Two days later, Ford decided to evacuate U.S. citizens from Lebanon.[21] He also went to Andrews Air Force Base in Maryland with Kissinger to meet the plane bearing the bodies of the slain officials. Ronald Reagan charged Ford with manufacturing a crisis for political gain, but the challenger failed to gain any traction with the allegation. Soon, Ford had secured the Republican nomination.

If Ford's biggest challenge was to heal the nation from the Nixon years, there was a mutual interest in laying down swords in the battle over the REA. "We benefitted from the Watergate scandal," said Wally Rustad, then a lobbyist for NRECA. "No one wanted to do anything because of the fight in 1973 over REA."[22]

As a freshman congressman on the House Agriculture Committee, Glenn English saw firsthand the friendship between President Ford and Texas Democratic U.S. Representative Bob Poage, a staunch electric co-op supporter. "President Ford was in no way hostile to the rural electric program," English said.[23]

In fact, the Ford administration in 1976 sent a statement to the NRECA Annual Meeting touting a $2.5 billion electric co-op loan program. Not that the Ford administration had suddenly embraced the New Deal. A week later, Agriculture Secretary Butz proclaimed, when it came to electrifying rural America, the "job is done."[24]

Perhaps Ford's most indelible stamp on the electric co-op program was his decision to keep David Hamil as REA administrator. Though Hamil had been associated with Eisenhower's Black Thursday and Nixon's Black Friday, he was an immensely popular figure within the rural electric program.

"David Hamil was clearly one of the best administrators we've ever had and was very committed to the mission of co-ops," said Rich Larochelle, who worked with Hamil at REA.[25]

In January 1975, Ford sent Congress a comprehensive 167-page energy proposal to deal with the nation's energy crisis. The bill called for doubling the nation's coal and nuclear power programs, but Democrats blocked its passage. Ford placed the blame squarely on U.S. Representative Tip O'Neill of Massachusetts, the soon-to-be Speaker of the House. O'Neill wanted a Democratic president, and he needed to make Ford look ineffective. "Stalling my energy proposals was one way to achieve the goal, especially when there was little public concern," Ford wrote. "People still didn't believe the energy crisis was real."[26]

In many respects, Gerald Ford's presidency, which lasted less than nine hundred days, was too brief to measure his support of electric co-ops. He had voted with Eisenhower against electric co-ops and listened to Nixon excoriate electric co-ops in the White House, but there was none of the vitriol of previous Republican presidents. When asked what he wanted to be remembered for as president, Ford replied without hesitation, "As a . . . nice person who worked at the job, and who left the White House in better shape than when I took it over."[27]

For the nine hundred Youth Tour representatives at the White House on a tragic summer day, President Ford was all that—and more. During one of the most memorable days of his presidency, Ford had given the students memories for a lifetime.

———— • ◆ • ————

In 1976, history may have been different if Ronald Reagan had not ventured into the thicket of TVA politics. Reagan, not Gerald Ford, may have faced Jimmy Carter in the 1976 presidential campaign. And some strategists believe Carter would have defeated Reagan in 1976 with the country eager to put the stain of Watergate behind them. As it was, Carter narrowly defeated Ford, winning 47 percent of the rural vote.

Carter had a political connection to rural electrification that few presidents could match. His father had been an electric co-op director, a man who often made the pilgrimage to Washington, D.C., to lobby for the REA. The OMB, however, cared little for Carter's life story, devising what NRECA considered a "secret plan" to undermine the REA loan program. Nearly two years into his term, electric co-ops were headed for a showdown with President Jimmy Carter.

In December 1978, a politically wounded Carter brought a group of electric co-op leaders to the White House. It was a pivotal meeting that presented Carter with a difficult choice: continuing an agency that had transformed his life or follow those who believed REA had completed its mission. Electric co-op leaders were on the edge of their seats, anxiously awaiting his decision.

President Jimmy Carter at a meeting of rural leaders on December 1, 1978. At the meeting, President Carter confronted a difficult decision on the future of the REA.

8

THE ELEPHANT IN
THE EAST ROOM

PRESIDENT JIMMY CARTER HAD MUCH ON HIS MIND. ON
December 1, 1978—a day for him that began at 5:30 a.m.[1] and
ended at midnight—he grappled with four American prisoners in
Cuba,[2] Strategic Arms Limitation Talks with the Soviets, normaliza-
tion of relations with China, and a harsh message from Egyptian
President Anwar Sadat about Middle East peace talks. Yet, over
lunch, as he prepared for a crucial afternoon meeting with two
hundred fifty rural leaders in the East Room, his thoughts turned to
something deeply personal. He recalled the day that lights came on
at his Georgia home.[3]

There was little time for reflection. Walking from the Oval Office
with Heywood Gay, executive vice president of the Georgia Electric
Membership Corporation, the president was brought back to the
harsh political realities of the White House.[4] His Democratic coalition was crumbling around him, and electric co-ops could soon be
joining the long list of aggrieved interest groups.

Carter was fifty-four-years old and in excellent physical condi-
tion, a president who could run a seven-minute mile. Politically,

however, he was in dreadful shape.[5] Labor was displeased with his failure to implement national health insurance. Congressional Democrats were rankled over his veto of water projects funding, a battle that Carter claimed left "deep battle scars."[6] Now he had to deal with nervous electric co-op leaders who had been crucial to his victory in 1976 and would be again in 1980. If anyone questioned the importance of the rural vote to Carter, they only needed to see the all-star cast assembled in the East Room.

Vice President Walter Mondale of Minnesota attended along with Agriculture Secretary Bob Bergland, Interior Secretary Cecil Andrus, and scores of other federal officials.[7] The meeting was the inspiration of Heywood Gay, whom White House memos to the president indicated is "a longtime supporter of yours."[8] White House Chief of Staff Jack Watson informed Carter, "Gay has increasingly become concerned about friction between the administration and persons in the rural electric field, many of whom were campaign supporters of yours."

While a series of new rural initiatives had been cobbled together for the meeting, it was a proposal led by one of the more obscure officials that dominated the discussion. Eliot Cutler, an OMB associate director, had been the lead negotiator behind a controversial plan to dramatically overhaul the REA.

The unease about this plan pervaded the East Room. Carter's advisers placed the most important guests up front.[9] Carter entered the room and followed his staff's instructions to shake hands "with those in the front row on both sides and in the middle." They specifically mentioned Partridge.

The White House staff was worried about NRECA. A year earlier, Don Smith, an incisive NRECA economist, had obtained the OMB internal strategy paper aimed at severely restricting the rural electrification loan program. "The whole objective of the paper," Smith said, "was to gut the REA."[10] Partridge read the memo, too, and on September 9, 1977, electric co-op leaders across the country would see a giant, red-lettered headline in the *Rural Electric Newsletter* that screamed: OMB SCHEME REVEALED.[11]

NRECA was also aware that Carter had asked for the REA study in preparation for his budget. "I can't believe that the president was aware that such a document existed when he asked for an 'objective study," Partridge had said. NRECA concluded the plan was "far less than objective and aimed at making the cooperatives more reliant on high-interest private loans for their capital needs."

The issue continued to fester. For several months NRECA attacked the study, questioning the sincerity of the authors, and claiming that the changes to the REA program would increase electric rates by nearly $100 per month. A White House memo to the president stated, "While every effort was made to conduct a comprehensive and objective analysis, intense political opposition to the study and any changes in the program has developed."[12]

President Carter knew he had to confront an issue that threatened his support in rural areas. Stepping up to a podium, basked in light from the giant chandeliers, Carter wasted no time reminding the audience of his history.

"I was thinking, during lunch, when I was contemplating coming over here to meet with you, that perhaps the most exciting and gratifying days of my life were when they turned on the electric lights in our house, when I was thirteen or fourteen years old, and when I was inaugurated as president." Flashing his trademark smile, he added: "I think even the days that followed turning on electric lights, everything was still pleasant. I can't say the same thing about being inaugurated as president." The crowd laughed. Then Carter turned serious.

"Electric cooperatives have always been close to me, and to my family, as you well know," the president said. "Those of you who know anything about my background realize this. The formation of the REA during the '30s opened up a new opportunity for an expanded and productive life."[13]

Carter's father had an aversion to much of FDR's New Deal, but he embraced rural electrification, quickly becoming one of the most influential electric co-op leaders in the region.[14] During his improbable run for the White House, Carter followed in his father's footsteps, speaking at an NRECA Annual Meeting and observing the NRECA resolutions process.[15] He knew the group's political power, and electric co-op leaders appreciated his background. When he took office, NRECA supported his focus on energy conservation but worried it tilted too far away from generation and supply in areas such as nuclear energy.

Few Americans knew as much about nuclear power as Carter. He had trained in the nuclear program at the U.S. Naval Academy under Admiral Rickover and told electric co-op leaders: "I still have a strong commitment to nuclear power. It should be, obviously, produced in a way that's safe, and we've done that in our country."[16]

Months later, Pennsylvania's Three Mile Island nuclear power plant would become a household name after a partial meltdown. Incensed by what he called "irresponsible scare tactics designed to terrify the public," Carter tried to calm the situation by touring the facility with his wife, Rosalyn, just days after the crisis. Prophetically, Carter wrote in his diary that the event "will cause severe damage to nuclear power plant construction."[17]

Carter also addressed the water projects controversy. A year earlier, he had pored over a U.S. Army Corps of Engineers cost-benefit analysis and eliminated what he criticized as "unnecessary dams and water projects that would cost billions of dollars and often do more harm than good."[18]

Electric co-op leaders considered these facilities necessary sources of power, and they challenged the president, running ads in *The Washington Post*: TORPEDO THE DAMS? NO. FULL SPEED AHEAD. These projects should not be built, Carter said, just because they were a pet project of a senior member of Congress.[19]

His time was running out in the East Room, but he had yet to tackle the future of the REA. For rural leaders, there was an ominous reference earlier when the president stated, "There may be times—when because of absence of communication or difference in technique or perhaps a time schedule—that we don't completely agree on how to address controversial problems . . ."[20] Electric co-op leaders were waiting in suspense. Carter knew it was time to take the issue head-on.

———— • ◆ • ————

Agriculture Secretary Bergland had a ringside seat that day, aware of what the president was going to say, but unaware that one day he would lead an organization represented in the room. His years with Carter would give a perspective into the inner-workings of the U.S. presidency that are unrivaled in the history of the electric co-op program.

If a Georgia peanut farmer was an improbable president, Bergland was an unlikely pick for agriculture secretary. He had grown up without electricity, watched an effort to establish an REA co-op fail in his community because the men "thought it was a hoax."[21] Then the women, he said, organized and the vote for the co-op won easily. He was later elected to Congress, and while he certainly had the qualifications for agriculture secretary, he was not part of Carter's so-called "Georgia Mafia." Bergland had an influential sponsor, however, in a fellow Minnesotan who just happened to be elected as Carter's vice president.

"Walter Mondale called me and asked me if there were any

conditions that I would join
the administration," Bergland
said. "I was stunned." Bergland
met with Carter in Plains,
Georgia. The two men quickly
developed a rapport. Carter
asked if he would agree to
a standard FBI background
check. Part of the background
check was an interview with
Bergland's mother. When the
FBI showed up at her door in
Minnesota, she thought her
son had robbed a bank.

Photo courtesy of the National Rural Electric Cooperative Association

NRECA General Manager Bob Bergland also
served in the U.S. Congress and as Secretary
of Agriculture under President Jimmy Carter.

Offered the post in late
1976, Bergland developed
a "high regard for Carter's
intellect and integrity," but not his communication skills. "He had
a shrill voice and his style did not work," Bergland said. "During a
speech, he would slide through the periods and stop at the commas."
Believing that the president needed "elocution lessons," Bergland
and U.S. Interior Secretary Andrus approached Jack Watson, one of
Carter's top aides. Watson reluctantly agreed to broach the subject
with the president. Weeks later, they asked Watson for a progress
report.

"You guys almost got me fired," Watson said. Carter wanted no
part of speech training. "This is how God made me," he told Watson.
Bergland also knew the president was in trouble politically. "The
first couple of years, it was a disaster. He got better at it, and by the
time he got to the third and fourth years of his administration, he
was getting better all the time."

———— · ◆ · ————

Now, Carter stood before the rural leaders in the East Room, completely aware of the volatile politics of the REA. He took the only course of action he could take. "I might also alleviate some concerns," the president said. "*There will be no proposal made to eliminate the REA loan program. There will be no proposal made to move REA out of Agriculture.*" Heads were turning now, and relief swept through the room. Carter had done what was necessary to keep the peace with an important constituency. "I think you know that Bob Bergland would not mislead you in any way," he added. "None of us have any inclination to mislead you. And when that kind of concern arises, it seems to fester like a sore, and needs to be nipped in the bud immediately."[22]

When he finished, after speaking twenty-one minutes, rural leaders "applauded like crazy," remembered Don Smith.[23] Carter had listened to OMB staff, who concluded, "We do not think it is advisable to ask the Congress to consider reforms of the program at this time, given the large number of more urgent items on next year's agenda."[24] At the meeting, OMB's Cutler said facetiously, "You aren't going to have OMB to kick around anymore."[25]

Carter then excused himself from the East Room. Defusing the REA issue was just part of his day. He had much more to do: meet with the prime minister of Egypt, get fitted for ski equipment, and have a photo taken with an up-and-coming Arkansas governor who had attended the meeting with rural leaders: Bill Clinton.

Soon, there would be a divisive primary challenge from U.S. Senator Ted Kennedy and a more difficult general election battle with Ronald Reagan. The map dictated Carter's every move. The 1976 presidential election had carved the country into neat slices: Ford had carried the West, while Carter had won the Deep South.

"In 1976, the key to my victory had been strong loyalty from my fellow Southerners," he wrote in his memoir, *Keeping Faith*. "To prevail against Reagan, it would be necessary for me to keep this support."[26] On October 31, three days after his televised debate with Reagan, Carter traveled to Florida, a crucial battleground state. It was Halloween, which was fitting, for the electoral nightmare was setting in. Carter had lost the final debate with Reagan, and undecided voters were breaking for the challenger. In the final political campaign of his life, Carter fought with the tenacity of the president he most admired, Harry S. Truman.

> **Many of you grew up like I did in the South. You saw your lives changed by Democratic administrations. They faced difficult issues. They made tough decisions. And almost always, the Republicans were there in opposition . . . Republicans were against the rural electrification program. They said that the power companies themselves ought not have any competition from those TVA dams that gave our farmers a better life.[27]**

His speech in Lakeland, Florida, sounded reminiscent of the 1948 Whistle-stop campaign, but history would not repeat itself. Carter still could not overcome double-digit inflation, skyrocketing interest rates, and the hostages at the U.S. Embassy in Tehran. Days later, Jimmy Carter would lose Florida and forty-three other states. Carter also received only 41 percent of the popular vote, the worst showing of an incumbent president since Herbert Hoover in 1932.

However, no president has—or ever will—write more eloquently about when the lights came on for a young boy in rural America. Just as Carter's work did not stop after he left the White House, his recollections of the importance of REA to his family are part of his legacy. "Had it not been for the REA program," Carter once said, "I would not be president, so I am thankful for it."[28]

———— ◆ ————

At the end of the Carter administration, 98.7 percent of the country was electrified, but many rural areas were beyond the reach of the rapidly expanding telecommunications industry. Home satellite television was beginning to take root, and electric co-ops started to take an interest in this new technology. The year 1980 also saw the death of Clyde Ellis. "It was apparent to all observers that during the darkest hours of battle, Clyde Ellis would stand and walk with a winner's confident stride," said Frank Stork, longtime head of the Association of Missouri Electric Cooperatives.[29]

Ronald Reagan was the first president since the advent of the REA who had only an abstract notion of electric co-ops, a combination of his big-picture style and his motion-picture background. Hollywood was a long way from rural America, and California's electric co-ops were bit players in the Golden State's giant energy scene, a role they gladly embraced.

Reagan had won overwhelmingly among voters in electric co-op service territory, and he promised during the 1980 campaign that any changes affecting REA "would be made with the advice and counsel of the rural electric leadership."[30] Weeks after he was inaugurated, with rumors abounding that the REA was on the chopping block, Bob Partridge requested a meeting with the president to remind him of those promises. The meeting never took place. Eight years later, as Reagan left office, electric co-op leaders were still waiting.

For NRECA, the Reagan years were "marked by arbitrary rule changes, the reluctance of presidential appointees to administer the REA Act as Congress intended, blackouts on information, wasteful, unproductive investigations . . . which attempted to show that the federal loan program was unnecessary."[31]

For Partridge, that also described the first months of 1981.

courtesy of the National Rural Electric Cooperative Association

President Ronald Reagan with Budget Director David Stockman. Electric co-ops
"had never gotten over the thrill of cheap electric power," Stockman wrote.

9

BELOW THE RADAR

RONALD REAGAN HAD NOT BEEN SWORN IN AS THE FORTIETH president and could not yet lay claim to the prime real estate at 1600 Pennsylvania Avenue. The work of fundamentally reshaping the federal government, however, was already under way and located across the street in the Blair House, a red-brick colonial building used by guests of the current president.[1] It was there that the president-elect's high command met in a room that conveyed serious business: nameplates, White House note pads, sharpened pencils, heavy water pitchers, and stewards pouring coffee for the major players of the incoming administration.

Vice president-elect George H.W. Bush was there, along with soon-to-be White House Chief of Staff James Baker, and Ed Meese, a top Reagan aide. But they were not the most important men in the room. That honor went to the man sitting next to President-elect Reagan. His name was David Stockman, the director of the Office of Management and Budget.

Brilliant, arrogant, and blunt, the thirty-four-year-old former congressman was known for his encyclopedic knowledge of federal programs and his zeal to enact supply-side economic policies.

Stockman had impressed Reagan during his role in debate preparation in the 1980 campaign, and had been rewarded with a job he
desperately wanted. Now he was, in his words, "surrounded by the
heaviest hitters in the nation's government."

Stockman outlined the deteriorating budget outlook, brandish-
ing a chart that showed the Carter administration had left a $58
billion budget deficit. "Damn it," Reagan exclaimed. "I knew they
were going to do this to us. It just proves what we've been saying all
along."[2] Stockman's message was clear. There would be "far more
sweeping and wrenching budget cuts than we had told the public
would be needed."[3] The president, according to Stockman, seemed
far above the detail work, but his support empowered the OMB
chief. "If the mess is really this bad, that's all the more reason we're
here," Reagan pointed out.[4]

Stockman now believed he had Reagan's blessing to go "forth
and do what I thought necessary to battle with the federal dragon."
He was prepared to eliminate a staggering number of federal
agencies. He'd placed a bulls-eye on the Economic Development
Administration, Amtrak, mass transit subsidies—and the REA.[5]
Stockman could barely contain his contempt for the REA and
electric co-ops.

"The whole countryside had been strung with electric wires by
1950, bringing the original mission of the REA co-ops to an end,"
Stockman contended. "But the co-ops had never quite gotten over
the thrill of cheap electric power."[6]

There were more meetings over the next several weeks, and a
dizzying array of charts and graphs. When the budget was finally
crafted, Stockman was pleased that they had targeted more than
three hundred programs to cut, reform, or eliminate. The REA was
at the top of his list.

These proposals, Stockman warned the president, were going

to cause political pain. There were groups that would fight hard to protect their turf. The president had been forewarned, and he never even flinched at the challenge ahead.

"No question about it," the president said. "It has to be done."[7]

So began David Stockman's war against electric co-ops as the president remained high above the fray. "Ronald Reagan was a big-picture guy," Glenn English observed. "Electric co-ops were way below his radar."[8]

In March, the president proposed to deny electric co-ops the right to borrow from the Federal Financing Bank and eliminated the REA 2 percent loan program. The White House staff was deployed to explain the fine print in the budget. Larry Kudlow, OMB assistant director, spoke to the CFC Board of Directors and outlined the rationale for the REA cuts. "We looked very carefully at the REA programs—the objectives of the programs—many years ago," Kudlow stated. "We decided that most of these objectives have been met and the time was long past when the government should be subsidizing REA."[9]

Partridge had another view. "There are going to be a lot of disappointed voters when they see their power rates increase with absolutely no effect on the budget."[10] NRECA's Don Smith calculated that under the Reagan proposal the average electric co-op consumer would pay nearly $34 more per month for electricity by 1986.

Electric co-ops were again under scrutiny. They were featured in *Newsweek, Time,* and *The Washington Post* and vilified as subsidized and antiquated. For the first months of 1981, it seemed as though every day was Black Friday.

The firewall NRECA had built on Capitol Hill was still standing, evidenced by the thirty-eight senators who signed a letter to the president, urging him to discontinue his assault on the REA. U.S. Senator Strom Thurmond took Stockman aside after a meeting at the White House. "Now we're all behind the president's program . . . but you take care of those REAs," Thurmond said.[11]

The Stockman plan was so bold that even Republicans on Capitol Hill doubted the Reagan budget, with the REA cuts, could be enacted. But everything changed on March 30, 1981, when Reagan took his budget sales pitch to the Washington Hilton. He was attempting to sell the deep budget cuts necessary to enact his broad economic program. "We must first get government spending under control," the president said to the AFL-CIO. "I propose cutting $48.6 billion from the federal budget in fiscal year '82. Now it's true these are the largest spending cuts ever proposed."[12]

Few people remember the president's message in his workmanlike, twenty-four minute speech. What people recall is that when the president left the hotel, a deranged gunman fired six bullets, one of them lodging an inch from the president's heart. Tragically, four people were shot that afternoon, including White House Press Secretary James Brady.

Reagan's popularity soared after the assassination attempt. He personally lobbied hundreds of congressman, his extraordinary charm and humor more than compensating for his lack of command of budgetary detail.[13] As he pushed his economic plan through Congress, attracting scores of Democrats, electric co-ops were in a perilous position. Their firewall was now in serious jeopardy of being overrun.

Then, things got worse. On Reagan's eleventh day in the hospital, an Oklahoma Republican named Harold Hunter was nominated as REA administrator, beating out other candidates considered too supportive of electric co-ops.[14] Hunter, a Polled Hereford rancher, had run against English for Congress in 1978—a race that English won convincingly. If Stockman needed help to destroy REA from within, Hunter was ready to oblige.

NRECA continued its grass-roots lobbying, stacking twenty thousand letters in the mailbox of one Republican congressman.[15] With bipartisan support of powerful legislators such as U.S. Representative Jaime Whitten, a Democrat from Mississippi, and Republican U.S. Senator Mark Andrews of North Dakota, NRECA fought to distinguish itself from the three hundred other programs on the chopping block.

Just 108 days after his inauguration, Reagan won his first budget victory in the House, a stunning legislative achievement. Sixty-three Democrats, including many electric co-op supporters, crossed over to vote for his economic plan. Reagan had rammed through bigger budget cuts than anyone imagined. The president's first budget was the only one passed by Congress virtually intact. Prior to the vote, Republican U.S. Senator Pete Domenici of New Mexico announced that a joint House and Senate Committee had accepted President Reagan's budget with one exception: the recommendation to cut the REA.[16]

NRECA's clout on Capitol Hill frustrated Stockman. In his estimation, "even the most blatant boondoggles we had proposed to cut or eliminate were producing stout champions, and each time I looked out the window, I saw more of them gathering, sharpening their blades."[17]

Electric co-op leaders had survived the initial onslaught against REA in 1981, baffled that they were not able to persuade White House officials that its proposals would result in no savings to the Treasury. Partridge believed that OMB's attacks on REA backfired, and members of Congress who supported the president parted company with him on electric co-op issues.

Partridge also worried that the OMB was likely to avoid its mistakes in 1982, which could make it "a more formidable foe in the future." In its 1982 report, *Congressional Quarterly* made it clear who was winning. *"The (Agriculture Appropriations) panel generally ignored proposed REA budget reductions, providing $400 million more than requested . . ."*[18] Stockman was undeterred.

In 1983, Partridge continued to preach resolve. "We may be a little tired of these battles, but I predict Stockman will learn that we're not only older, we have gotten tougher in these last two years." That year, Partridge also announced his retirement after leading NRECA for sixteen years. He had worked with four different administrations, guiding the association through some of its most memorable battles. In future years, Partridge was a mainstay at NRECA meetings and remained exceedingly popular with NRECA membership and staff.

His successor was former Carter Agriculture Secretary Bob Bergland. After leaving the Carter administration, Bergland served as president of Farmland Industries, the nation's largest farmer cooperative. He believed in rural development and that electric co-ops were an organizing force in their communities. Now he went to work to convince Reagan administration officials of the merits of electric co-ops, even if they didn't want to listen. "We never had one meeting with Reagan," he recounted later. "But we had many meetings with Harold Hunter."[19]

The name Harold Hunter sparks an intense reaction from electric co-op leaders who worked with him in the 1980s. The collegial, often friendly relationship between the REA administrator and electric co-op leaders became fractured and adversarial. Bergland said Hunter would mostly "sputter and fume" when NRECA made their arguments about the importance of the REA. NRECA professionals such as Wally Rustad and Wallace Tillman also dealt with Hunter.

"He was a hale and hearty guy," Rustad said, "except when he was trying to put us out of business."[20] Tillman called Hunter's tenure "the lowest point in the rural electric program."[21]

None of this scorn rubbed off on Ronald Reagan. The president remained a popular figure with electric co-op leaders by sheer force of personality. In straw polls held at NRECA regional meetings during the 1984 presidential campaign between Reagan and former Vice President Walter Mondale, the president carried twenty-five states to Mondale's eighteen.[22] It frustrated NRECA leaders who battled the administration each day. "NRECA stopped publishing the results," NRECA lobbyist Rich Larochelle said, not wanting to embolden a White House whose objective was the end of rural electrification.[23]

Mondale attended an NRECA regional meeting and upbraided Reagan for failing to keep his promise to consult with electric co-op leaders. "In each of the past four years, this administration has proposed deep cuts in the REA program, and there were no consultations at all."[24] Mondale touted his perfect voting record on electric co-op issues and expressed hope that the health of rural America would be a major issue in the upcoming presidential debate. The debate, though, barely touched on rural issues.

That fall, Reagan sent a taped message to the NRECA regional meetings, stating without a hint of irony, "Rural leaders emerged and began the formidable task to form rural electric and telephone cooperatives that today serve America so well."[25]

Reagan won the 1984 presidential election in a landslide, taking forty-nine states and dominating the rural vote. The administration had only four years left to dismantle the REA and they went to work again. REA staff was tasked to research how many "urban" co-ops were served by the REA, and, allegedly, how many brothels were served by Nevada electric co-ops.[26] The OMB also released a report that concluded, "Power from REA-backed nonprofit cooperatives recharges the golf carts at Hilton Head Island."[27]

Nothing seemed to work, and in 1985, Stockman departed OMB unable to take down the REA. "Four years and about 15 billion wasted REA dollars later," he wrote, "the fight would still be going on."[28] No one told Hunter of the futility of their proposals. "REA has not been of significant help whatsoever to rural America," Hunter testified to the U.S. House Agriculture Committee in 1986.

For Hunter, the House Agriculture Committee was a safe haven compared with the House Government Operations Committee, where U.S. Representative Glenn English chaired an agriculture sub-committee. English relentlessly grilled Hunter, accusing the Reagan administration of "wanting to bleed REA dry and whittle it down to nothing." Hunter did not argue the point.

In the latter part of Reagan's second term, the administration abandoned their proposed phase-out of REA and instead attempted to change the mission of the program. "The Reagan people had learned you cannot go head-on against the REA," English said. "Instead it was guerilla warfare."[29] Congress was unconvinced, and the White House failed to find a champion on Capitol Hill to advance their REA reform legislation. They had, by all accounts, simply given up on Stockman's original mission. However, they found another one.

In 1983, the Grace Commission recommended selling the federal Columbia River dams, an important source of wholesale electricity for Pacific Northwest electric co-ops.[30] Stockman embraced the idea, and offered a stunning trial balloon before Christmas in 1985: selling the Bonneville Power Administration and three other Power Marketing Administrations (PMAs).

Bergland called the proposal "absurd," and committed the full weight of NRECA against the proposed PMA sale.[31] Republican

U.S. Senator Mark Hatfield of Oregon said the proposal would happen "over my dead body" and helped pass legislation prohibiting even the study of the idea. The proposal to sell the federal Power Marketing Administrations was put in a drawer, where it waited patiently to be dusted off. A decade later, the drawer would be opened again.

Bergland later reflected on the Reagan years, using a farming metaphor. "The Reagan years were a tough row to hoe. The whole crowd thought the government had no business being in the electric business. We just endured."[32]

In 1981, Larry Kudlow had been part of the assault on electric co-ops as David Stockman's associate at OMB. By 2012, Kudlow was a popular broadcaster and reporter with the cable business network CNBC, and a paid speaker before a group of more than one thousand electric co-op leaders in a Hilton Hotel ballroom in midtown Manhattan. The politically conservative audience enjoyed his observations about Reagan's philosophy on cutting taxes, rolling back spending and regulations, while rebuilding the military. "The president spoke on four or five points and that's all he ever said," remarked Kudlow.[33]

Toward the end of his presentation, the moderator reminded Kudlow of his days with Stockman in the 1980s and OMB's attack on rural programs. Kudlow was taken aback. "Oh Lord," he said. Acknowledging that he had lost track of the issue, Kudlow replied, "Stockman was trying to clip away REA, just as he was clipping away at everything else." It seemed much had changed in thirty years, for both electric co-ops and Kudlow. "I'm not here to tear down programs," he said. "If something works, keep on doing it."

———— • ◆ • ————

Electric co-ops were hoping for a political détente with the
new president, George H.W. Bush. He carried forty states against
Massachusetts Governor Michael Dukakis in 1988, piling up big
margins in rural America along the way. As a U.S. envoy to China,
CIA director, and vice president, he had operated far outside the
orbit of electric co-ops, save for a speech to the Electric Cooperative
Youth Tour in 1983. Expectations were low, as evidenced by a
headline in an electric co-op publication that read: BUSH NOT AS
BAD AS REAGAN.

As expected, foreign policy dominated Bush's presidency. On
January 16, 1991, CNN broadcast the first shots of the Gulf War into
America's living rooms. President Bush was watching along with the
First Lady and Reverend Billy Graham as cruise missiles pummeled
the Iraqi capital of Baghdad. Weeks later, the war was over and
CNN's coverage had revolutionized TV news. However, there were
many rural Americans not served by cable providers, and who could
not watch CNN during the Gulf War.

In an attempt to provide their consumers with the same television programming as those in the cities, many electric co-ops had
invested in satellite television. At the time, the cable industry was
charging satellite providers up to 500 percent more than local cable
operators for the same television programs.[34]

In 1992, Congress passed the Cable Television Consumer
Protection and Competition Act to give satellite television much
needed help. "If this bill is signed into law, rural satellite dish
owners will finally have access to competitively priced television
programming and services," Bergland said. "The president should
sign this bill."[35]

However, in October 1992, in the midst of a bitter presidential election, Bush vetoed the bill on behalf of the cable industry. The future of satellite television was in jeopardy. History was again coming full circle for electric co-ops. Now, they had to override a veto by a White House that had never lost a veto fight, defeating a president who could not afford to lose.

George H.W. Bush greeting Youth Tour students in 1983.
In 1992, electric co-ops and President Bush clashed over satellite
television legislation in the midst of a presidential campaign.

10

THE VETO OVERRIDE

L IBERATING KUWAIT FROM SADDAM HUSSEIN WAS THE
signature achievement of the Bush presidency and sent his
approval ratings into the stratosphere. By the fall of 1992, a lingering
recession had sent his ratings crashing back to earth. Bush's diary
said it all: *I can make it; I can outhustle Clinton; out work him; out
jog him; out think him; out campaign him; and we'll win. But it's an
ugly spot in the road right now.*[1]

Voters had pivoted hard from international affairs to economic
issues. In a political instant, the president had become an underdog
against Democratic Arkansas Governor Bill Clinton. A third-party
candidate, Texas businessman Ross Perot, was draining Republican
and Independent votes. And a month from the election, the
Democratic Congress had found the ultimate issue to embarrass
him with voters: cable TV rates.

The growth of the cable television industry had brought com-
plaints of poor customer service and subscriber price increases
three times the rate of inflation.[2] Congress believed it had found a
solution by re-regulating the cable industry. In 1992, both the U.S.
House and Senate passed the Cable Television Consumer Protection

and Competition Act.[3] The Bush administration opposed cable re-regulation legislation, protesting that "the bill illustrates good intentions gone wrong, fallen prey to special interests." On October 3, 1992, President Bush vetoed the bill and dared Congress to override it. Based on his track record sustaining vetoes, Bush had to like his chances.

The nefarious-sounding "special interests" that Bush highlighted in his veto message included electric and telephone co-ops. In 1992, cable was available in 60 percent of American households, but millions of Americans were still beyond the reach of cable lines. Bergland believed that access to television was similar to bringing electricity to the rural areas in the 1930s. In 1986, electric and telephone co-ops decided to bridge the technology gap, forming the National Rural Telecommunications Cooperative (NRTC).[4]

NRTC was led by Bob Phillips, a former co-op attorney from Kansas with a sweeping vision of the nascent satellite TV industry becoming a true competitor to cable in rural areas. Technology was advancing from the giant C-Band satellite dishes in a farmer's backyard to a pizza-pan-sized direct broadcast satellite dish mounted on any roof. "The smaller dishes will make satellite TV more efficient and affordable for rural consumers," Phillips said.[5]

In May 1992, NRTC and two hundred fifty of its utility members served seventy thousand rural TV subscribers and had committed to raise $250 million for a budding company called DIRECTV.[6] But Phillips knew satellite TV would only become a true competitor to cable if consumers could get access to the programs carried by the cable companies without being gouged.

The cable legislation prohibited this overcharging with so-called "program access" provisions. NRECA and NRTC supported "program access" because it leveled the playing field. President Bush made his opposition clear in his veto message, stating, "Another special interest provision would put the federal government in the position of dictating to cable companies to whom and at what price they could sell their programs."[7]

Getting the "program access" amendment into the bill had required a bit of hubris. The provision had been deleted in the U.S. House Energy and Commerce Committee because of opposition from cable and from the committee's formidable Democratic Chairman, U.S. Representative John Dingell of Michigan. NRECA had to find a way to amend the bill, but it needed someone to challenge Dingell on the House floor. Dingell, a congressional heavyweight, was not easily rolled. NRECA found a taker in colorful Louisiana U.S. Representative Billy Tauzin, a legislator who knew satellite issues better than almost anyone in the U.S. House. After showing up on the House floor in the nick of time after playing basketball, Tauzin offered the amendment. It passed the House and later survived the Senate. Now it had to overcome President Bush's veto.[8]

It is not an exaggeration to say the future of the satellite TV industry was riding on the vote. If the president's veto was overridden, Phillips said the law would "finally end the cable industry's discrimination against the rural television marketplace . . ."[9] There was much at risk for NRECA, too. "If we lost the vote, then NRECA would lose some of its luster," said Larochelle. "It had implications for all our programs, including REA and the PMAs."[10]

If the arguments were on their side, the politics were not. Since the 1930s, nine U.S. presidents had one-quarter of their vetoes overridden by Congress. In 1991, Bush had vetoed twenty-one bills without being overridden.[11] The Bush White House engaged in a sophisticated veto strategy that was highly coordinated with the Republican congressional leadership. One Democratic leader lamented Bush's veto success, "We have fallen into a trap thinking that if we don't have a two-thirds vote, we should do nothing."[12]

The veto override on the cable legislation was scheduled in the House and Senate for Monday, October 5. On Sunday, Bush used the full trappings of his office, inviting eight Republican senators to breakfast for some arm-twisting.[13] He really needed their support. It was a month before the election, and he couldn't afford to look weak.

Powerful interests aligned on both sides, strange inside-the-Beltway coalitions that form for a common purpose and then quickly disband. One side included broadcasters, consumer groups, and electric co-ops seeking broader access to programming. The White House aligned with the cable industry and the Motion Picture Association of America, whose members included Hollywood studios providing television programs.

The cable industry had a $10 million advertising budget to defeat the bill. The Motion Picture Association had Hollywood star power, led by charismatic former LBJ staffer Jack Valenti, who curried favor by inviting legislators to watch movie premieres at his plush Washington, D.C., theater.

Money was at stake in the veto override, but so perhaps was a presidency. *The New York Times* stated that "debate over cable television prices has become subordinate to the broader theater of the election. The Democrats have been eager to portray the president as an enemy of consumers; Republicans say the Democrats are beholden to special interests . . ."[14] U.S. Senator Al Gore of Tennessee, who was Clinton's vice-presidential nominee, alleged that Bush was owned "lock, stock, and barrel" by the cable industry.[15]

Steering clear of partisan sniping, NRECA kept its focus on rural legislators. Carolyn Herr Watts, one of the lead NRECA lobbyists on the issue, recalled how electric co-op leaders laid the groundwork during the NRECA May Legislative Conference. "We put on neon blue-and-pink buttons that read *TV for Rural America*," she said. The buttons, the brainchild of NRTC executive Jeff Almen, "spooked the cable guys," said Herr Watts.

NRECA also circulated a chart showing where the money flowed if satellite TV could not get access to fair prices from the likes of Disney, HBO, and CNN. The chart showed money leaving consumer's pockets in rural America toward Hollywood and Atlanta, home of CNN.

On the day of the override vote, the White House took no chances. Chief of Staff James Baker held another breakfast meeting with a select group of senators to keep the troops in line. One legislator remarked that the cable legislation seemed like the only thing the White House cared about. Administration lobbyists appeared to lurk behind every pillar in the U.S. Capitol. No one was sure of the outcome. "It's going to be close," said U.S. Senator Trent Lott of Mississippi. "I wouldn't want to bet on it."[16]

Electric co-op leaders were taking no chances either. Calls and letters from electric and telephone co-ops poured in from across the country. The Senate was scheduled to vote first, and NRECA felt confident given that rural interests tend to be overrepresented in the chamber, with North Dakota's vote counting the same as New Jersey's.

GOP Minority Leader Bob Dole of Kansas led the debate for Republicans on the Senate floor, stressing loyalty to the White House. "Sustain the president's veto," Dole pleaded with his colleagues. "He hasn't asked for much."[17] Other Republicans, such as South Carolina U.S. Senator Strom Thurmond, had another view. "I think this bill is good for the consumers of America." Voting 74 to 25, the Senate overrode the president's veto with twenty-four Republicans—a majority of the GOP—voting against their president.

Now came the hard part. The urban-dominated House of Representatives was scheduled to vote later that evening. NRECA lobbyists fanned out, concentrating on rural Republicans, working the phones and using old-fashioned shoe leather. "I was camping out at people's offices," Herr Watts said. Taken aback by the Senate vote, the cable industry was also lobbying furiously.

In its last major veto fight more than three decades before, NRECA had watched victory slip away when Republicans rallied around President Eisenhower. If the cable legislation devolved into a partisan squabble, history would repeat itself, and the satellite TV industry would pay the price.

As the U.S. House took up the veto override, U.S. Representative Steve Gunderson, a Wisconsin Republican, took to the microphone. "This is not a vote to embarrass the president," he said. "This is a vote to support our constituents."[18] It was also a positive sign when Chairman Dingell spoke in support of the legislation. "This is not a partisan issue," he said. "The Consumer Federation of America says it will save the American public $6 billion a year." Dingell then listed the organizations that supported the override: "The National Association of State Attorneys-General, the National League of Cities, the rural co-ops . . ."[19]

To defeat the president, electric co-ops would need 290 votes if all the members voted—an extremely high wall to climb. An electronic board on the back wall of the House chamber would tally the votes. In fifteen minutes, NRECA lobbyists would know if the letters, phone calls, and personal visits to offices had paid off. The House chamber was hushed and filled with anticipation. The initial vote did not look good for the future of satellite television. House Republicans loyal to the president were voting early. The margin was too close to override the veto. Then, the numbers began to shift.

Not surprisingly, an overwhelming number of Democrats voted to override the president. The electronic board revealed something else: A large number of Republicans were now voting against the president's position. U.S. Representative Craig Thomas of Wyoming, a former electric co-op statewide manager, voted to override. So did U.S. Representative Bill Emerson, a Missouri member of the House Agriculture Committee. When the gavel came down at 9:47 p.m., seventy-seven Republicans had opposed the president. Electric co-ops had needed 290 votes. The final tally was 308 to 114. They had defeated Bush with eighteen votes to spare.

Congress, for the first time, had overridden a veto from President Bush. In the House chamber, the Democrats began chanting "four more months," a reference to how much time they believed President Bush had left in office.[20] "President Bush's veto was anti-rural as well as anti-consumer, but fairness and competition won," said Bergland.[21]

The New York Times wrote, "The cable vote was both a setback for the president at a time when his struggling campaign for reelection hardly needs any reverses, and an apparent sign of his eroding political influence."[22]

But what would have happened if the cable television lobby had prevailed? "If we had not overridden the veto, there would have been few program choices and minimal subscribers," said Bob Phillips. "It would have put direct broadcast satellite off for a decade, if ever."

With a level playing field to acquire programming, NRTC led the effort for co-ops to invest in new, cutting-edge small-dish technology through DIRECTV. In 1994, a satellite was launched, and millions of rural Americans who had been beyond the reach of cable had access to comparable television programming.

Former NRTC executive Jeff Almen wrote, "After years of tough trench warfare, impossible odds, and formidable adversaries—big cable, large media concerns, Hollywood interests . . . and the White House—Bob Phillips and NRTC, NRECA and the rural utility industry had made a dramatic contribution to rural America."[23]

DIRECTV is now in twenty million homes.

The cable television battle with the Bush administration was an anomaly. On balance, the Bush years lacked the contentiousness of the Reagan years toward the electric co-op program, but followed the pattern of low-balling the REA budget, only to see Congress restore the funds. The slash and burn tactics of David Stockman were nowhere to be found. "George Bush, Sr. was a decent guy, a sensible moderate," remembers Bergland. "He had his hands full with Russia and other issues."[24]

During the Bush administration, the Congress also passed the Energy Policy Act of 1992 and the Clean Air Act amendments. The Bush policies on environmental and energy issues were generally in line with NRECA, including one that would soon be at the forefront. The president resisted international demands for emissions caps and compliance deadlines to curb carbon dioxide emissions, a major issue for electric co-ops relying on coal-fired generation. It seemed as if a new issue had emerged in the public policy arena: global climate change.

———— · ◆ · ————

In 1992, the country was looking for change in the White House after twelve years of Republican rule. The agent of change was William Jefferson Clinton, the governor of Arkansas. During the election, Clinton was not about to cede rural voters to President Bush. Upon seeing the draft of his 1992 convention speech, Clinton realized there was no reference to farmers, so he ad-libbed a line, "We're losing our farms at a rapid rate, and he has no commitment to keep family farms in the family, but I do."[25]

Electric co-op leaders were impressed with Bill Clinton. During the campaign, Clinton also charged that the Reagan and Bush administrations "completely neglected the needs of rural Americans. The way they have run the REA is conclusive proof."[26] He won the presidency, in part, because he neutralized the rural vote, capturing 43 percent in a three-way race with Bush and Perot. "I think he has great respect for us and realizes the contribution we make to the state," said Carl Whillock, leader of the Arkansas electric co-op statewide association and a man who helped Clinton launch his political career. Whillock conceded, though, that Clinton didn't "know much about the program nationally."[27]

As President Clinton entered the U.S. House chamber for his first State of the Union speech in February 1993, electric co-op leaders were eager to learn more about this young, dynamic president. They had many questions. When it came to rural electrification, was he an old-school Democrat in the mold of FDR, Truman, and LBJ? What type of new rural initiatives would he propose?

They did not know it yet, but the answer to these questions could be found in Bill Clinton's own handwriting in the margins of his speech.

President William J. Clinton had a surprise in store for electric co-ops
during his 1993 State of the Union Address.

11

SACRED COWS IN
THE MARGINS

O N FEBRUARY 17, 1993, AS PRESIDENT BILL CLINTON
stood at the lectern in the U.S. House, it seemed as though the
world was watching. No speech before a joint session of Congress
had attracted such a share of the viewing public: Sixty-six million
Americans had tuned in to watch the forty-five-year-old president
discuss his vision for the country.[1] Electric co-op leaders were
watching, and they were excited. Clinton reminded many
Americans of John Kennedy, but unlike JFK, the new president was
from the small town of Hope, Arkansas. Clinton understood rural
issues. The personal connection with Carl Whillock didn't hurt,
either. Whillock had Clinton's ear, and he'd make sure the president
knew the importance of REA and federal hydropower.

Early in the speech, the president spoke of the national debt,
telling the audience that if America stacked its debt in thousand-
dollar bills, "the stack would reach 267 miles" into space.[2] As a sym-
bolic gesture of how serious he was about fiscal discipline, Clinton
had invited Alan Greenspan, chairman of the Federal Reserve, to sit
next to First Lady Hillary Clinton in the gallery. "It is not enough to

simply cut government," Clinton said. "We have to rethink the way that it works."

There was nothing particularly compelling about the speech until the president said his deficit reduction plan will be "real deficit reduction, using the independent numbers of the Congressional Budget Office." In the House chamber, Republicans snickered.

Turning to the Republican side of the aisle, Clinton, a serial ad-libber, fired a fastball right back at them. "Well, you can laugh my fellow Republicans, but I'll point out that the Congressional Budget Office was normally more conservative in what was going to happen and closer to right than previous presidents have been." The Democrats cheered. "A direct hit," wrote *Washington Post* columnist Mary McGrory.[3] The Republicans appeared as if they had been turned to stone.

Forty-four minutes into the speech, the president was prepared to demonstrate he was a different kind of Democrat.

> *As I said earlier, my recommendation makes more than one hundred fifty difficult reductions to cut federal spending by a total of $246 billion. We are eliminating programs that are no longer needed, such as nuclear power research and development. But many of these programs were justified in their time, and a lot of them are difficult for me to recommend reductions in, some really tough ones for me personally.*[4]

Focusing his attention on the Republicans, the president slowed his cadence and brought his hands close to his heart.

> *I recommend that we reduce interest subsidies to the Rural Electrification Administration. That's a difficult thing for me*

to recommend. But I think that I cannot exempt the things that exist in my state or my experience, if I ask you to deal with things that are difficult for you to deal with. We're going to have no sacred cows except the fundamental abiding interest of the American people.[5]

The normally dignified House chamber roared with approval, now sounding more like the rowdy give-and-take common in the British Parliament. Behind Clinton, Vice President Gore and U.S. House Speaker Tom Foley of Washington led a standing ovation of both Democrats and Republicans. The boisterous cheers forced the president to pause and enjoy the moment. His reference to "sacred cows" had struck a chord with both political parties. Democrats rallied around their new president, while Republicans were not about to let Clinton highjack their mantle of a leaner government. There was another sound, too, one that could not be heard in the House chamber. Across rural America, jaws were dropping.

Congressman Glenn English was on the House floor, astonished at what he had just heard about the REA.[6] Whatever the president proposed would be assigned to his subcommittee on the Agriculture Committee. He intended to find out more about this proposal and how it originated. Meanwhile, in the comfort of their homes in the Washington, D.C., area, NRECA lobbyists were not cheering. "I've been waiting my whole career for a president to mention REA in the State of the Union, and it happened," said NRECA's Wally Rustad. "But he wants to cut its funding."[7]

No one saw it coming. Clinton's reference to the REA was not in his prepared text. That made it all the more shocking. "Watching that felt like getting punched in the gut," recalled Rich Larochelle, knowing moments after Clinton's reference to REA, the world had changed for the storied New Deal agency.[8] Stephan Petry, a veteran

NRECA lobbyist, agreed. "The president's words," he said, "moved the game over to a different stadium."[9]

It was just twelve words in a presidential speech, but such words, delivered by a Democratic president in a hostile budget climate, could create undeniable momentum in Congress for reform.

REA would be under the microscope again, precipitating the full force of electric co-op leaders and their allies on Capitol Hill to salvage the program.

History had shown it could be done. But all of the strategy, lobbying, and ceaseless negotiations to achieve these ends would occur later. The question that evening for shell-shocked electric co-op leaders and supporters—watching a Democratic president from a rural state call for cuts in the REA—was more fundamental, more basic.

How exactly, they wondered, did this happen?

———— ◆ ————

The discussions had started twenty-one days before around a mahogany table in the Roosevelt Room, a large White House conference room decorated with pictures and artwork of Theodore Roosevelt and FDR. On January 29, nine days after the inauguration, the president and his advisers commenced an extraordinary series of meetings to draw up an economic program. The meetings went late into the night, with the smell of pizza in the air.

Clinton presided over the meetings, in shirtsleeves, his eyeglasses sliding down his nose, immersing himself in the details of budgeting, determined, in his own words, to "understand the human impact of our decisions."[10] Soon, they were examining rural programs line by line. Clinton recounted the sessions, "Most of the team wanted to cut farm supports and other rural programs, which they thought were unjustifiable."[11] The centrist Progressive Policy

Institute, with close ties to Clinton, had already called REA an "obsolete institution."[12]

There were few voices in the room for rural America, other than the president himself. His OMB Director was Leon Panetta, the former House Budget Committee Chairman from California; Bob Rubin, a New Yorker from the Goldman Sachs investment firm, was named chair of the National Economic Council. The group also included the brusque Lawrence Summers from Harvard University.

But it was the whip-smart, diminutive deputy OMB director, Alice Rivlin, who wanted to swing the big budget axe. "Mr. President," Rivlin said, "I've got a slogan for your reelection." Pivoting off the signature line from his campaign, the pledge to "end welfare as we know it"—she proposed that Clinton announce: "I'm going to end welfare as we know it for farmers."[13] Clinton did not like the sanctimony in her voice.

"Spoken like a true city dweller," he snapped. "Farmers are good people," he reminded his team. Leaning dramatically across the table, Clinton directed his ire at Rivlin. "I know we have to do these things. We're going to make these cuts. But we don't have to feel good about it." A chill fell over the room. Bill Clinton may have taken no joy in the decision, but the decision had been made. And electric co-op leaders were oblivious.

The REA was now going to be Exhibit A in the White House's argument for cutting outdated federal programs. The White House understood the political sensitivity. Gene Sperling, the deputy director of the National Economic Council, wrote a memo to the president listing the REA as an example of a spending cut that needed careful language. "Making government work for the next century," Sperling wrote, "means ending funding for programs that don't work and updating policies and programs that were designed to meet the needs of an earlier era."[14]

Few who followed the Clinton presidency would be surprised that chaos ensued on the day of Clinton's economic speech before the Joint Session of Congress. The speech was to be delivered in five hours, but the president was not happy with the text. "This is just spend and spend," he said.[15] Revisions were made. Clinton practiced the speech in the White House theater. The interest rate subsidy for REA was one of the few specific spending cuts in the draft speech. However, Clinton still didn't like the tone. He decided to cut the line about the REA.

After another practice session, the president huddled with advisers. More specific spending cuts were needed, they told him. Clinton considered his options. I'll include the reductions to the REA, Clinton told them. He said he would ad-lib something about how painful this would be in Arkansas. It was now time for the president to leave for Capitol Hill to give the speech.

Clinton continued to make edits during the limousine ride from the White House, and even as he waited outside the House chamber. The last minute-edits precluded the REA reference from being in the advance text given to members of Congress. The line about the REA and its impact on Arkansas was a notation in the margin.

David Kusnet, his speechwriter in 1993, pointed out that "about 20 percent of this speech was ad-libbed or spoken from his own handwritten notes—not from the final text distributed to the news media and on his teleprompter."[16]

Twenty years earlier, President Richard Nixon excoriated the REA during a televised White House press conference, but President Bill Clinton shined perhaps the brightest lights ever directed upon the agency. It was also good politics for Clinton, no matter what he said. He had demonstrated he could break with Democratic ortho-doxy and go after a New Deal program. The heavy lifting would be done by Congress. It was in Glenn English's court now.

That is why English wanted to learn more about the administration's decision-making process. He expressed concerns about the REA cuts to Vice President Al Gore during a meeting with the Democratic caucus. Gore replied that Tennessee electric co-ops had told him they didn't need the program anymore. "That's not what I'm hearing from my Oklahoma co-ops," English told the vice president.[17] English checked with the Tennessee co-ops and learned they had no idea where Gore had gotten his information. The damage, however, was done.

The Washington Post also took note of President Clinton's remarks, devoting an entire series on the REA, claiming it was "an agency caught between two eras." The reporters hoped to "shed light on how programs live and die on Capitol Hill."

Electric co-op leaders had no intention of letting REA die. "We didn't much care for those [Bush] plans," said Dennis Hill, executive vice president of the North Dakota Association of Rural Electric Cooperatives. "And we're not big fans of this one, either."[18]

Meanwhile, President Clinton kept the pressure on. The day after his speech to Congress, he traveled to St. Louis and said he was forced to cut programs that were "close to my heart." He added, "the [REA] serves a lot of people in my state and yours. But America is 100 percent electrified now, and we ought not have the full subsidy continued from all the rest of the people who get their electricity from someplace else."[19] What Clinton conveniently overlooked in his speech was that the *someplace else* included investor-owned utilities enjoying healthy federal tax breaks.

Clinton had found a winning issue, one that allowed him to demonstrate that he, too, was feeling the pain. He told the Cleveland City Club that after his proposal to cut REA, "I may get shocked instead of light when I go home."[20]

Electric co-op leaders were not laughing when they learned the size of the cuts. The Clinton administration proposed cutting

$545 million from the REA budget over five years. On February 23, Bergland wrote members of Congress, making clear that electric co-ops would not be a scapegoat. "The administration's budget, however, has unfairly singled out rural electric cooperatives and the twenty-five million people they serve."

In mid-March, the action moved to the third floor of the Longworth House Office Building and the U.S. House Agriculture Committee. English, the Chairman of the Environment, Credit, and Rural Development Subcommittee with jurisdiction over the REA, called for a crucial hearing on Clinton's proposal. Invited witnesses included Bergland and Clinton's friend Carl Whillock.

Whillock's role at the hearing was to make the case that electric co-ops were the least subsidized of any in the utility sector.[21] But there was a political element, too. In 1974, Clinton was making his first attempt at elective office, running for Congress against a popular Republican incumbent. Whillock, a venerable Arkansas political professional who knew everyone, opened his card files and campaigned with Clinton across the district. Though Clinton narrowly lost that race, he never forgot what Whillock had done for him. Yet, even Whillock was unaware of Clinton's plans for REA.

English set the tone of the hearing in his opening statement. "I've noticed that some critics of the REA program, whenever we do have successes in economic development, point to these successes as the reason to eliminate the program," English said. "They're economic development programs that provide jobs, that provide growth, that provide opportunities for rural America, and that's what the bottom line is all about."[22]

But the negative publicity had taken its toll. Republican U.S. Representative Jim Nussle of Iowa pointed out that shows such as *60 Minutes* had made it hard to defend REA back home. "I have a difficult time saying, "Hey, REA is one of these things I can't cut.""

English, frequently interviewed for these news shows, did not believe this was a valid argument. "They're interested in a good story," English said. "They're not interested in the facts."

NRECA attempted to sway public opinion with an ad in influential newspapers that showed a historical photo of a laughing FDR, with the tagline, "FDR would laugh all over again." The ad noted, "The arguments against the REA haven't changed since the New Deal."

The ad was clever, but the Congress of 1993 was not the Congress of 1936 or even of 1973. Bergland admitted to *The Washington Post* that it was difficult to sell the REA to a younger generation of politicians. Few members of the 101st Congress remembered what it was like to stand in line at the outhouse door, pump water, and wash clothes by hand. "The leadership of the '30s is all gone," Bergland said. "It changes the politics of the REA and I understand that."[23] Time, it seemed, had caught up with electric co-ops and the REA.

There were no pep rallies in the Mayflower Hotel or fiery speeches by supporters urging electric co-op leaders to "throw beer bottles" if necessary to protect the REA. "We went to Democratic leaders, and they said REA had to change," remembers Larochelle.[24] Bergland concluded that one important change was to rebrand REA.

While many in the electric co-op membership believed the "REA" name was sacrosanct, it became clear a new image for the program was necessary. REA, for all its success, had become good fodder for those who wanted to eliminate what they perceived as outdated programs. Whatever they called the agency, English believed there was an appropriate federal role for the government to aid small electric co-ops. "It's a job that's never going to be done," English concluded.[25] Then he and Democratic U.S. Senator Howell Heflin of Alabama worked out the details of an updated co-op loan program.

The U.S. House and Senate Agriculture Committees worked closely with NRECA and produced a bill that reduced the cost of the REA lending program. The 2 percent loan program was abolished, creating a 5 percent hardship loan available to co-ops serving the poorest and most remote areas. The changes also allowed electric co-ops the chance to play a larger role in rural development. Soon thereafter, the U.S. Department of Agriculture reorganized and a new agency—the Rural Utilities Service—was born.

On November 1, 1993, a day he was consumed with lobbying for the North American Free Trade Agreement (NAFTA), Bill Clinton signed H.R. 3123, the Rural Electrification Loan Restructuring Act. In his statement, the president said, "We should no longer hear about wealthy electric and telephone borrowers that receive government loans at extremely low interest rates."[26]

The Washington Post reported, "Without fanfare, President Clinton has signed into law a bill that reforms the REA—the New Deal agency that has long been a target of government-waste critics, who say it has outlived its usefulness." The *Post* recounted what had happened after Clinton's "sacred cow" speech before the Congress: "The law is the culmination of nine months of aggressive lobbying, detailed negotiations and compromise among administration officials, lawmakers, and advocates for the nation's electric and telephone co-ops." The new law, the *Post* reported, "follows *a little-noticed* promise Clinton made to the nation . . . when he singled out the REA in his State of the Union address as an example of where cuts could be made to reduce the deficit."[27]

There was nothing *little-noticed* about the speech for electric co-op leaders.

"Most of us would have been more comfortable if no change had been required, but that was not an option," Bergland said.[28] English agreed. "We enhanced the overall utility effort . . . and we

were able to bring about some savings," he said. "We made lemon-
ade from lemons."[29]

—————— •◆• ——————

Bill Clinton was not yet done taking on the pillars of the electric
co-op program. The Democrats were shellacked in the 1994 mid-
term elections, losing both the House and the Senate. The Clinton
administration, which had been portrayed as big-spending, big-
government liberals, was looking to demonstrate a commitment to
a smaller, leaner government. They accomplished this by ripping
a page from Ronald Reagan's playbook. A White House from the
party of FDR, Truman, and Kennedy, that had helped build massive
multi-purpose federal hydroelectric projects across the country,
now wanted to sell them off.

In 1995, President Clinton's budget proposed the sale of three
Power Marketing Administrations: Southeastern, Southwestern, and
Western Area Power Administrations. To hear President Clinton
explain it, he wasn't sure about the cost savings. "When they brought
it to me, I said I don't necessarily think this is going to save money,"
he said.[30] He went ahead with it anyway, creating another dangerous
minefield for electric co-ops. The sale of these assets could lead to
rate increases for millions of consumers served by the more than
six hundred electric co-ops that relied on the federal hydroelectric
dams for electricity.

NRECA was thrust into another legislative battle, against a
gathering army of both political parties. Yet it wasn't going to be
Bob Bergland's fight. In 1993, he announced his retirement. A
man who had grown up on what he called a "poor, rural, poverty-
stricken, subsistence" farm had become a congressman, cabinet
secretary, and a leader of a major trade association.[31] Mark Glaess,

general manager of the Minnesota Rural Electric Association, said that Bergland "not only saved the REA loan program, he increased funding and reignited the passion for the program."[32]

In January 1994, Bergland gave way to the new CEO, Glenn English. The NRECA Board of Directors had watched English in action on Capitol Hill and knew he had the capacity to take electric co-ops into the next century. While he did not seek the job, English was ready for a new challenge.

Intense, focused, but with good humor, English had cut his political teeth in California under Jesse "Big Daddy" Unruh, the legendary speaker of the California Legislative Assembly. English understood the levers of power. A former football player, he also knew politics was a contact sport. Witnesses before English's sub-committees often found themselves sputtering after his tenacious, prosecutorial-like questioning. He had a unique combination of rhetorical and political skills and, above all, he played to win.

The "PMA sale fight of 1995" would be a serious test of English's skills. Not only had the Clinton administration proposed to sell off the PMAs, House Republicans were upping the ante on the president. House Speaker Newt Gingrich implored his House colleagues to cut as many programs or agencies as they could. The U.S. Department of Energy was targeted for closure. No department or agency was too big or small to eliminate.

In February 1995, English wrote President Clinton urging him to reverse his proposal to sell the PMAs. The sale, English argued, would result in "immediately increased electric rates and a smaller return to the taxpayer."[33] NRECA then unleashed a furious lobbying campaign against the proposal, sending thousands of letters and postcards to Congress. The campaign began to find traction, particularly on a key committee with jurisdiction over the PMAs.

U.S. Secretary of Energy Hazel O'Leary testified before the

House Energy and Water Subcommittee and found a less than receptive audience. Her message reached White House Chief of Staff Leon Panetta. She informed Panetta, "The members expressed concern about and in some cases opposition to" the PMA sale plan.[34]

In May, English testified before the House Resources Committee, which would soon vote on the PMA sale plan. In a tense, combative hearing, English reminded lawmakers that electric co-ops pledged to buy hydropower in the 1940s and '50s at a higher rate in order to help the government pay for constructing the dams. English told the committee, "Now, the investor-owned utilities, with their deep pockets, made possible in part because of the $5 billion a year in tax breaks they get from U.S. taxpayers, want to bid up the price for the federal power marketing administrations."[35]

The PMA sale issue dogged Clinton at a town hall event on June 1, 1995, in Billings, Montana. After an electric co-op member questioned him about the PMA sale, Clinton responded, "I will approve this only if you do two things, in our proposal. One is to put a lid on how much rates can go up—which makes it less attractive, obviously to private utilities. And two, there has to be an extraordinary effort to let public power authorities buy the capacity first." The president concluded, "And if it doesn't work out, then, in my opinion, it shouldn't pass at all."[36]

If Clinton was having second thoughts, House Resources Committee Chairman Don Young was not. Facing tremendous pressure to meet Speaker Gingrich's budget targets, Young and U.S. Representative John Doolittle offered an even more radical idea: selling off the Southeastern Power Administration (SEPA), including the lakes and dams—to the highest bidder. SEPA marketed electric power generated at reservoirs operated by the U.S. Army Corps of Engineers. Nearly five hundred electric co-ops and municipal utilities relied on the electricity from the dams. The reservoirs were also popular with thousands of anglers and boaters.

NRECA was stunned at the audacity of the proposal. There was little chance that electric co-ops could outbid deep-pocketed investor-owned utilities. And what would happen to the thousands of sportsmen who enjoyed these recreation areas? Would the new owners put a fence around the lake, or charge a fee for access? The House Resources Committee leadership had few answers, but they still moved ahead with the vote.

NRECA lobbyists found Republican House members who had opposed the sale suddenly wavering out of fear of Speaker Gingrich. Despite intense lobbying, the sale of SEPA passed the House Resources Committee on a heartbreaking 19–18 vote. It was a disappointing defeat for electric co-op leaders. The Republican staff who drafted the PMA sale legislation celebrated, but a committee professional who respected NRECA's clout gave them a warning. "This is a long way from being over," the staff member said.

But it was over, and very soon. As electric co-ops regrouped, preparing to fight the battle on the floor of the U.S. House, events began spiraling out of control for Speaker Gingrich.

The full ramifications of this proposal had been discovered not only by consumers who would see their electric rates rise, but also the sportsmen who had been tipped off by NRECA that they may lose access to their favorite lake or reservoir. Bad policy for electric co-ops was becoming bad politics for Republican candidates. The sale of SEPA became a defining issue in the Kentucky gubernatorial campaign. Larry Forgy, the Republican candidate for governor, absorbed a withering attack from sportsmen. Speaker Gingrich realized he had a problem that threatened his party's majority hold on the Congress.

In a hastily arranged press conference, Gingrich buried the legislation and announced, "The lakes will not be sold, the dams will

not be sold, and no fishing rights or public access will be interfered
with." It was too late, however, for Larry Forgy, who lost his election.

The PMA sale proposal became a campaign issue in other close
elections in 1996. Gingrich and the Republicans took the brunt of
the criticism as Clinton quietly cut his losses. President Clinton
knew the politics of the issue were not helpful to his reelection.
In 1996 he told *RE Magazine*, "Due to the concerns expressed by
electric cooperatives . . . my fiscal year 1997 budget did not include
any PMA transfer proposal."[37]

Clinton won a second term in 1996, improving his showing
among rural voters to 47 percent. He even brought Carl Whillock to
Washington, D.C., as an adviser at the Department of Agriculture.
Having an ally that could whisper in Clinton's ear became an invalu-
able asset at keeping OMB at bay. "They were afraid of Carl," said
Wally Rustad, then the director of NRECA's Government Relations.
"I think his access was much more than people thought."[38]

Bill Clinton had an eventful second term. Lost in the impeachment debate over his affair with a White House intern was a bal-
anced budget with the Congress. Electric co-ops were able to avoid
deep cuts in their programs because of strong allies on Capitol
Hill, including a co-op-friendly chairman of the House Agriculture
Committee, Oregon U.S. Representative Robert F. Smith. But there
were new issues on the horizon, outside the jurisdiction of the
Agriculture Committees.

The "restructuring" of the electric utility industry was under
way, opening a path for large industrial customers to shop for lower
electricity prices. The proposal made most electric co-ops wary.
President Clinton told electric co-op leaders, "We seek again to gain
the benefits of competition in electricity markets without compro-
mising other important policies such as fairness to all classes of
electricity customers."[39]

Rich Glick, a senior policy adviser to the Secretary of Energy during the Clinton years, said electric co-ops always had to be accounted for in policy debates. "NRECA was extremely potent and Glenn English was a good leader," said Glick. "You had to worry about them."[40]

As the new millennium—and another presidential election—approached, there was much to worry about for electric co-ops beyond the RUS loan program and the PMAs. Some co-ops were growing at an amazing rate. In addition to the traditional rural and remote areas of the country, electric co-ops were serving fast growing counties around Atlanta, Tucson, Austin, and Washington, D.C. No matter who served in the White House, electric co-ops would soon find themselves facing new and more complex issues than they had ever faced before.

The electric utility industry was changing, and so were the politics.

———— • ◆ • ————

In 1998, Vice President Al Gore was invited to speak at the NRECA Annual Meeting in Nashville, Tennessee. But Gore's staff balked, fearing that he would elicit boos before the more than ten thousand rural leaders in his home state. Instead, Gore delivered the speech from a studio in Washington, D.C., via satellite.

Whether it was Gore's position on global climate change or other environmental issues, the episode highlighted a seismic shift in the relations with electric co-ops and the Democratic Party. An electric co-op program born and raised by Democratic presidents was now part of the "red state" America dominated by the Republicans. And rightly or wrongly, the man who was ultimately the Democratic nominee for president didn't feel comfortable enough to show up to an NRECA annual meeting in person. Vice President Gore won the popular vote in 2000, but ultimately lost the election by 537 votes in the state of Florida.

During the 2000 election, Texas Governor George W. Bush won big across rural America. Federal hydroelectric projects became a sleeper issue in the campaign. Karl Rove, the architect of George W. Bush's victory, hammered Gore in the Pacific Northwest for supporting efforts to "destroy the region's dams, a source of jobs, and green power."

President Bush came to the White House committed to work on national energy legislation, and he ultimately achieved that goal. The story of the Bush era is not that in 2005—after four years, countless congressional hearings and intense high-stakes negotiations—a small group of electric co-op leaders joined the president in an Albuquerque, New Mexico, auditorium for the signing of the most significant energy legislation in decades.

It is a story of how electric co-ops came to be in that auditorium at all.

Electric co-ops were key players in the passage of the Energy Policy Act of 2005. President George W. Bush with New Mexico Senators Pete Domenici and Jeff Bingaman.

12

PUNCHING ABOVE
THEIR WEIGHT

PRESIDENT GEORGE W. BUSH LOVED TO MOUNTAIN BIKE.
In August 2005, he planned to do a lot of it while staying at his ranch in Crawford, served by Heart of Texas Electric Cooperative. It wasn't necessarily a vacation; he'd simply moved the West Wing twelve hundred miles.[1] He'd still receive daily intelligence briefings and check in regularly with advisers. On August 8, 2005, however, he was going to use the ranch as a base for travel on one of the most important days of his presidency.[2]

He was traveling to Albuquerque to sign the Energy Policy Act of 2005. Less than a year after winning a second term (where he had won rural voters by nineteen points against Democratic Massachusetts U.S. Senator John Kerry), the president was going to celebrate the defining domestic achievement of his second term.

Sandia National Laboratory, the venue for the bill signing, was a showcase for innovation and a nod to New Mexico's powerful U.S. Senators, Republican Pete Domenici and Democrat Jeff Bingaman, who played crucial roles in the bill's passage as members of the Senate Energy Committee. The energy legislation's four-year journey was more of an ultra-marathon than a sprint. President Bush may have left the sausage making to the U.S. Congress, but he had provided the leadership to make it happen. This was undeniably his day.

After a quick tour of the Sandia facility, President Bush entered an auditorium with all the trappings of a choreographed event, including a light-blue banner with the presidential seal that read *Energy Security for the 21st Century*.[3] The most important prop was on the desk itself, a copy of the 1,724 page Energy Policy Act.

"It looked bigger than a big-city phone book," marveled Keven Groenewold, CEO of the New Mexico Rural Electric Cooperative Association.[4] With both of his state's senators holding leadership positions on the Energy Committee, Groenewold took his lobbying responsibility seriously. He was now seated among VIPs, comprised of energy industry leaders who helped get the bill across the finish line.

English and NRECA lobbyist Chuck Penry were also invited to the ceremony, representing the electric co-op grassroots. English had whipsawed around Capitol Hill, testifying before the many U.S. House and Senate committees fighting for jurisdiction over the legislation. An exceptionally nimble congressional witness, English often frustrated legislators who disagreed with electric co-op positions. He was masterful at framing issues and rarely conceded an argument. At one hearing, an opposing congressman paid him the ultimate compliment. "I know better than to ask Mr. English a question," he said with a smile.

Electric co-op leaders were pleased to be inside the room that day in New Mexico, part of a successful coalition supporting the president. The legislative outcome, however, would have been much different without the grass-roots assistance of electric co-op leaders. Groenewold had a bird's eye view of how he ended up invited to a heavily secured national lab that day, only feet away from President Bush.

"We had to punch our way in," he explained.[5]

————— • ◆ • —————

George W. Bush had learned the hard way in Texas that electric co-ops could be an immovable object if legislation treated them unfairly. In the late 1990s, a company named Enron pushed the concept of "retail wheeling"—essentially opening the retail side of the electric utility industry to competition. Texas had caught deregulation fever, but electric co-ops had helped shelve legislation to deregulate the electric utility industry. And Governor Bush was not pleased.

"We were the fly in the deregulation ointment," remembered Mike Williams, CEO of the Texas Electric Cooperatives.[6] One Saturday, Governor Bush summoned Williams to his office and let him know his displeasure. An experienced former utility regulator, Williams was unapologetic about the electric co-ops' position on the issue.

The litmus test for Texas electric co-ops was whether legislation kept electricity affordable, and power supplies reliable for their consumers. The legislation, as proposed, had failed the test. Ultimately, a bill passed the Texas Legislature that better reflected electric co-op priorities. By that time, George W. Bush had grander plans. Soon he would come to Washington, D.C., and try his hand at energy legislation on a national scale.

Just after being inaugurated in 2001, President Bush asked Vice President Dick Cheney to chair a task force developing a national energy strategy.[7] Cheney's staff went to work, meeting with interest groups in Washington, D.C. Several organizations, including the Sierra Club and Judicial Watch, filed suit, demanding the White House release the lists of everyone they met with during the development of the energy strategy. The Bush-Cheney administration felt strongly they had the right to consult with anyone without revealing names. A legal battle ensued that went all the way to the U.S. Supreme Court.

Eventually, the list of who met with the Cheney Task Force was made public. It revealed that NRECA had one session with the Task Force. Andrew Lundquist, Cheney's point man on energy, came to NRECA's headquarters for a meeting with the Rural Electric Statewide Manager's Association. The session, while constructive, was not worthy of a Supreme Court case. Lundquist spent more time discussing the light motion sensors in NRECA's building than revealing any important details of the energy plan. When Tom Jones, a well-respected statewide manager from Arizona, urged the administration to protect the PMAs, Lundquist was noncommittal.

Within three months, the report was released, a timeline Cheney called "light-speed by government standards."[8] Cheney said the report made "recommendations to modernize conservation, modernize our energy infrastructure, increase energy supplies, accelerate the protection and improvement of our environment, and increase our nation's energy security." Congress now had a blueprint for action.

For the most part, English liked what he saw in the plan.[9] The recent California energy crisis had galvanized the nation, and the electric utility industry was receiving unprecedented attention. English informed electric co-op members in July 2001, "President Bush's plan moves the country in the right direction by helping focus attention on key issues of energy supply, energy delivery, and energy conservation."

The politics of energy did not favor electric co-ops. There were certainly other groups with better White House connections. During his time at Yale, Bush had roomed with Tom Kuhn, who went on to be the CEO of the Edison Electric Institute (EEI), the trade association for investor-owned utilities.[10] Large power companies had raised bundles of cash for Bush, while NRECA had stayed neutral in the presidential election.

It wasn't that NRECA couldn't play the money game. Its political action committee, the Action Committee for Rural Electrification (ACRE), consistently ranked in the top fifty in the nation for donations to Congress. ACRE membership had doubled on English's watch, but he saw a more compelling opportunity. Few groups outside of electric co-ops were legitimately focusing attention on how energy policy would affect the consumer. This was never more apparent than with the California electricity crisis, where massive power shortages, blackouts, and skyrocketing energy bills had exposed the dark side of retail wheeling—and of Enron. Electric co-ops had played a major role in killing deregulation discussions on the national level, pointing out that consumers in rural areas would be the biggest losers in the scheme.

In 2001, the U.S. House was also moving at light-speed on energy legislation, passing a comprehensive energy plan just before the August congressional recess.[11] The U.S. Senate was beginning to take action when they returned in September, but the legislation took a tragic detour on a warm, brilliant late summer day in the eastern United States.

———— • ✦ • ————

On September 11, 2001, President Bush was reading to second-graders at a Florida school, already aware that a plane had hit the North Tower of the World Trade Center in Manhattan. At 9:05 a.m., he was still reading when Chief of Staff Andy Card whispered to him: "A second plane hit the second tower. America is under attack."[12]

In western Pennsylvania, Rich Bauer, the general manager of Somerset Rural Electric Cooperative (REC), like millions of Americans, watched television coverage of the situation at the World Trade Center and the Pentagon. Shortly after 10 a.m., electric co-op business intruded.[13] There was an outage call in Shanksville, a small town in Somerset REC's service territory. A co-op line crew responded just as information came in that an aircraft was down in the area. Bauer hopped in a truck to survey the scene. What he found in the field that day he will never forget. "But I wouldn't have bet that it was an airliner," he said. "There wasn't enough debris to be something big."

President Bush was also getting a report of a commercial jet down somewhere in Pennsylvania.[14] He had authorized the military to shoot down aircraft, if necessary, but had no firm information. He asked Cheney, "Did we shoot it down, or did it crash?" He wondered if he had ordered the death of innocent Americans. Nobody knew. Bauer, for his part, only knew that a three-phase power line in a reclaimed strip mine had been incinerated.[15] Soon, both Bauer and the president would learn the powerful story of how United Flight 93, bound from Newark, New Jersey, to San Francisco had crashed into the field at 580 mph.

They would learn of the heroism of the passengers who fought to take back the aircraft from hijackers by storming the cockpit. The 9/11 Commission determined that the intent of the hijackers was to crash the airliner "into symbols of the American Republic, the Capitol, or the White House."[16] The report concludes they were "defeated by the alerted, unarmed passengers of United 93." President Bush wrote, "Their act of courage ranks among the greatest in American history."[17]

As a result, a small electric co-op in Pennsylvania played a role in one of the most unforgettable days in American history.

While the country grappled with how to help, Bauer believed that Somerset REC had, by a quirk of fate, "the ability to do something."[18] In the short term, the co-op supplied coats to FBI agents who had traveled to Shanksville unprepared for the autumn Pennsylvania chill. Bauer and his team also installed scores of meters and breaker boxes—electrifying, free of charge—a burgeoning city of trailers and RV's hauled to the scene to investigate the crash and provide support.

State and federal agencies descended on the area, including the Pennsylvania State Police, FBI, CIA, and National Transportation Safety Board. The real challenge occurred later when Bauer was notified that President Bush would be visiting the crash site to meet with families of the victims.

Bauer and his team were asked to provide electricity for the president's visit, but there was one specific request that posed operational challenges. Absolutely no electric facilities could be visible, a difficult engineering feat for a barren field. Bauer, an engineer, personally hooked up a transformer a hundred yards away through the nearby woods. The surreal nature of the activity was not lost on him. "I put a meter on the backside of a pine tree," Bauer said, "for the president of the United States."

———————— • ◆ • ————————

The terrorist attack against the United States was among the many detours for energy legislation during the Bush years. Disputes over oil drilling in the Arctic National Wildlife Refuge and other issues had derailed the bill. But Capitol Hill veterans who flanked President Bush at Sandia National Laboratory had finally shepherded it through the Congress. President Bush thanked everyone who had worked to make this day possible.

"I appreciate Pete Domenici's leadership on this bill," said Bush. "When he makes up his mind to do something, it is hard to stop him."[19] English agreed with President Bush's assessment of New Mexico's senior Senator. In spring 2003, Domenici, as the Chairman of the Senate Energy Committee, had initially crafted an energy bill NRECA could not support. Electric co-ops were faced with an imposing challenge. Either change Domenici's mind, or oppose an energy bill gathering nearly unstoppable momentum. Looking back, NRECA had no idea how quickly the window was closing. In May 2003, they had three days to change Domenici's mind.

That month, the Senate Energy Committee had passed an energy bill containing a weak exemption for small utilities from Federal Energy Regulatory Commission (FERC) jurisdiction.[20] NRECA believed a strong, ironclad "small-utility exemption" was needed to protect electric co-ops from a blizzard of paperwork and expensive attorneys that would be needed to meet the impending FERC regulations. NRECA Senior Regulatory Counsel Rich Meyer called FERC regulation the "sword of Damocles" hanging over small electric co-ops.[21] Ultimately, it could result in higher rates for consumers and businesses.

Groenewold and Penry met with Domenici and requested that he substitute NRECA's stronger "small-utility exemption." Domenici listened politely, but he had made up his mind. "I'm sorry, I can't put this in for you," he said.[22] He believed his legislation struck the right balance, and the electric co-op provisions would jeopardize the committee's work. Domenici was exceedingly fair, however, and he cracked the door a bit, offering to stand aside if electric co-ops could demonstrate enough strength to get their provisions into the bill on the Senate floor.

The ultimate test of strength was at hand. Overwhelming force was necessary to defeat the chairman of the Energy Committee, particularly a veteran, battle-tested legislator like Pete Domenici. If they failed, then NRECA would have no choice but to oppose the bill, a position English made clear: "We will not ask senators to vote for an energy bill that includes electricity provisions that extend more regulations over cooperatives . . ."[23]

The cavalry, however, had arrived. Nearly three thousand electric co-op leaders descended upon Washington, D.C., in early May for the 2003 NRECA Legislative Conference. The rally had become a linchpin of electric co-op lobbying efforts. English took full advantage of this veritable army, imploring electric co-op leaders at their legislative briefing to "roll-up their sleeves" and go to work on Capitol Hill. English then proceeded to roll up his shirt sleeves, much to the delight of the crowd.

English also gave them a mission: find legislators to support an amendment on the Senate floor. Electric co-op leaders deployed to Capitol Hill, determined to find a champion brazen enough to challenge Domenici. It did not take long.

Soon, Minnesota statewide general manager Mark Glaess convinced Republican U.S. Senator Norm Coleman of Minnesota to take up the challenge. Dave Wheelihan, CEO of the Montana Electric Cooperatives' Association, persuaded U.S. Senator Conrad Burns to join the battle. In addition, Republican U.S. Senators Lindsay Graham of South Carolina, Saxby Chambliss of Georgia, and Jim Bunning of Kentucky all offered to help. It was an embarrassment of riches. Senators of both parties were approaching Domenici on the Senate floor, informing him they supported NRECA's amendment.

Finally, Domenici had heard enough and relented. After a meeting with English to work out the details, the stronger "small-utility exemption" provisions were amended into the legislation without a bitter, divisive battle on the Senate floor. The three-day NRECA

Legislative Conference earned electric co-ops a new level of respect that carried through the rest of the energy bill debate. For Penry, it was about political muscle. "The chairman knew we had the votes," he said.[24]

"The electric co-ops were extremely successful players in the debate," said Lisa Epifani, a key Domenici aide and energy expert who helped write the bill. "I know that because other groups were annoyed that co-ops got not half of what they wanted, but all they wanted."[25]

As electric co-ops were winning a victory in the energy bill, the rural electrification program was also losing a great friend as Bob Partridge passed away in June 2003 from leukemia.[26] "His life was this program," said Don Smith, who worked closely with Partridge during many landmark battles.[27] Missouri electric co-op leader Frank Stork wrote, "[Bob] Partridge not only worked to electrify rural America, he had gained informal recognition as 'rural electrification personified.'"[28]

At the Sandia National Laboratory, President Bush was preparing to sign the bill, but he first outlined the electricity provisions that had been fought over for the last several years.

> The bill removes outdated obstacles to investment in transmission lines in generating facilities. The bill corrects the provision of the law that made electric reliability standards optional instead of mandatory. Most of you consider it mandatory that the lights come on when you flip a switch. Now the utility companies will have to consider it mandatory, as well.[29]

The crowd enjoyed the one-liner and while there were also provisions to encourage renewable energy and nuclear power, electric co-ops also endorsed the bill for what it didn't do. "We started with a renewable portfolio standard and mandated retail wheeling and slowly things got whittled away," noted Jay Morrison, an NRECA lawyer who advised English during the energy policy debate.[30]

"The bill I sign today is a critical first step," President Bush declared. "This bill is not going to solve our energy challenges overnight . . . I'm confident that one day Americans will look back on this bill as a vital step toward a more secure and prosperous nation that is less dependent on foreign sources of energy."[31]

The Energy Policy Act of 2005 was signed at 11:47 a.m. The president was proud of what he had done. "I had worked with Congress to promote alternatives to oil, including biofuels, hybrid and hydrogen vehicles, natural gas, clean coal, and nuclear power," he later wrote.[32]

English believed it was a remarkable achievement for electric co-op leaders across the country. "If it were not for our grass-roots lobbyists—the people back home—and the legislators who listened carefully to them, we wouldn't be celebrating this victory."[33] The staying power necessary to finish the job was also remarkable. The battle with Nixon over REA had taken five months; Bill Clinton's REA reform effort transpired in less than a year. Combined with the effort to push retail wheeling, the energy policy debate that culminated that day in New Mexico had taken *nine years.*

"It wasn't how much strength you could bring to bear on a particular day," English reflected. "But more about remaining steadfast and grinding away."

The *National Journal,* a respected voice of politics in Washington, D.C., wrote that electric co-ops "punched above their weight" in energy policy battles. And electric co-ops had finally won grudging respect from a Republican administration.

"The demographics had changed, and the White House was more comfortable with us," English said.[34] With friendly RUS administrators at the helm, including former NRECA President Jim Andrew of Georgia, the RUS loan program grew exponentially. Of course, there were still areas of disagreement. Instead of attempting to privatize the PMAs as Reagan and Clinton had proposed, Bush attempted to raise the rates on the power sold to so-called "market rates." The proposal went nowhere.

In August 2005, with the Energy Policy Act signed and a victory in his pocket, the president returned to his Crawford ranch. Meanwhile, Rick Haile, the manager of Heart of Texas Electric Cooperative, attempted to meet the challenges of serving the president and his entourage. "It kept us pretty busy," Haile said. George W. Bush returned the favor. "He's down-to-earth and friendly to the guys who worked out there," Haile said.[35]

The president looked forward to getting on his mountain bike, tearing around the trails, and hopping in the pool. Even Lance Armstrong was coming to Crawford for a bike ride. There were still reminders of his day job. Iraq War protestors stood on the road outside his ranch. Later that month, on Tuesday, August 24, 2005, Bush began paying attention to a tropical storm gathering force over the Bahamas as it zeroed in on the Gulf Coast. It was initially dubbed Tropical Depression Twelve.[36]

The National Weather Service soon named it Katrina.

AFTERWORD

DUSTING OFF THE PLAYBOOK

"This program was born in politics and will die in politics.
And I vowed it would not die on my watch."

FORMER NRECA CEO GLENN ENGLISH

T HE *WASHINGTON POST* REPORTED THAT IN 2011, AN IOWA
electric co-op employee named Janell Cheek met with a
Republican contender for president.[1] "There's a good shot I might
become the next president of the United States," the candidate said
as they met in a bank conference room. "It's not a sure thing but
a good shot." The candidate was interested in the electric co-op
business model and he peppered Cheek with questions. "Does coal
come in by rail from Pennsylvania?" he asked. "Do you have a trade
system for SOx and NOx?"

We know now that the candidate, former Massachusetts
Governor Mitt Romney, was off-base with his prediction. However,
his interest in electric co-ops is laudable, and a testament to an
inspired effort by the Iowa Association of Electric Cooperatives
to put electric co-ops back on the radar screen for future U.S.
presidents. Brian Kading, executive vice president of the statewide

Then Senator John F. Kennedy at an NRECA Board Meeting in 1958, as he prepared for his presidential campaign. "I notice we haven't had too many presidential candidates at our board meetings lately," said former NRECA CEO Glenn English.

association, knew the state's celebrated presidential caucus gave electric co-ops a chance to make a memorable first impression.

"We can meet all these candidates and do something to make them remember us," Kading said. Tapping into their potent grass-roots organization, the "Caucus Project" launched in 2011 as Republican presidential hopefuls swarmed the state. Wearing distinctive bright green shirts with the words "Rural Power" emblazoned on the front, a team of electric co-op leaders showed up at seventy different events with one hundred different people, asking the candidates one basic question: "What is your solution to provide affordable, reliable power?" The co-op leaders were so omnipresent that former U.S. Senator Rick Santorum remarked at one meeting, "The green shirts are here again."

"We tried to be everywhere," Kading said. "Our people enjoyed it." They invited all the candidates to their annual meeting and while many sent videos, former U.S. House Speaker Newt Gingrich appeared in person. Given Iowa's major role in winnowing the presidential field, the co-op Caucus Project appears to be a cost-effective strategy to educate potential nominees—or future presidents— about electric co-op issues.

The green shirts, however, are a long way from the glory days of FDR, Truman, and LBJ. Much has changed since electric co-op leaders like Clyde Ellis strolled into the Oval Office and counseled the president about the need for more hydroelectric dams. The country is long since electrified. Today, the issues are more complex, the politics more divided.

The Caucus Project was not yet under way in 2008 when a relatively junior Illinois U.S. Senator named Barack Obama rocked the political establishment, winning the Iowa Caucus on his remarkable ascent to the White House. Obama's meteoric rise to the presidency and urban base in Chicago made him an elusive target for electric co-op leaders to establish a connection before he became a national figure.

However, there have been other urban senators who reached out to co-op leaders because they saw the political upside. A young, charismatic senator's appearance at an NRECA Board Meeting in 1958 is still a point of pride for electric co-op leaders. "John Kennedy didn't attend the board meeting because he cared about electric co-ops," Glenn English said. "He wanted their support for president." It is also a cautionary tale. "I have noticed we haven't had too many presidential candidates show up at our board meetings lately," English added.

In his final years as NRECA CEO, English focused on maximizing the political potential of electric co-ops. He revamped the association's resolution process to make clear the position electric co-ops were taking on key issues. He also made winning the "hearts and minds" of electric co-op consumers a theme of NRECA's 21st Century Committee, a group dedicated to looking at the future "purpose" of electric co-ops.

These actions stemmed from the controversial and bitter 2009 fight in the U.S. House of Representatives over "cap and trade" legislation to combat global climate change. As Democrats, led by U.S. House Speaker Nancy Pelosi, drafted climate change legislation behind closed doors, electric co-ops found themselves ignominiously left out of the process. The so-called "Waxman-Markey" legislation, which was designed to reduce carbon emissions by 17 percent by 2020 from 2005 levels, was weighted heavily in favor of investor-owned utilities that participated in the negotiations.

Electric co-ops that relied on coal-fired generation for their power supply were put at a serious disadvantage under the complex cap and trade formula. English and his government relations team, with the help of conservative "Blue Dog" congressional Democrats, mustered enough support to save electric co-op consumers a staggering $3 billion over the next decade if the bill was enacted.

After being shut out of the legislative process, NRECA did what it has done since its inception, building support and getting the best deal they could for their members. But few in the electric co-op community were celebrating. Speaker Pelosi had the votes, and the bill narrowly passed the U.S. House of Representatives. The bill ultimately died in the Senate and many Democratic House members who supported the legislation were defeated in the 2010 election. For English, it was not only a close call, but a wake-up call for the electric co-op program.

NRECA CEO Jo Ann Emerson will undoubtedly write new chapters in electric co-op history, just as the four previous leaders have done over the past seventy years. The hiring of Emerson, an

NRECA CEO Glenn English. Few could match his rhetorical ability
behind a podium or before a congressional committee.

experienced, savvy Missouri congresswoman put electric co-ops
back in the news in late 2012. *Politico*, a popular source of inside-
the-Beltway news, concluded that, "Although in its heyday from
the 1950s through the 1980s, NRECA had incredible political
clout, decades later, lawmakers, congressional staffers, and other
trade groups still know to pay attention when the co-ops voice
their concerns."

Whether NRECA's heyday is over is a debatable point, and there
will be plenty of opportunities to prove *Politico* wrong. The fights
over the REA described earlier in this book will yield to new battles
over climate change, the use of coal-fired generation, national
renewable-portfolio standards, cyber-security, and many other
issues that FDR never envisioned in the 1930s.

No matter what the issue, it is time, English argues, to "roll up our sleeves and dust off the playbook." It's hard to argue his point. It is a playbook that successfully partnered co-ops with U.S. presidents to electrify a nation, and helped provide electricity for one hundred million more people around the world.

The playbook also brought modern telecommunication services to rural America, helped supportive presidents win elections, and even tried to help them win wars. The playbook called for battling presidents over policy and not partisanship; for staying united, and most importantly, never forgetting the magic of the family who came up the hill and saw, for the first time, the lights shining inside their home.

NOTES

Preface

1. "President Sets Up Rural Power Unit," *The New York Times*, May 12, 1935.
2. Day by Day, Franklin D. Roosevelt Presidential Library and Museum.
3. D. Clayton Brown, *Electricity for Rural America* (Westport, Connecticut: Greenwood Press, 1980), p. 44.
4. Brown, *Electricity for Rural America*, p. 22.
5. "President Sets Up Rural Power Unit," *The New York Times*.
6. Jean Edward Smith, *FDR* (New York: Random House, 2007), p. 324.
7. Brown, *Electricity for Rural America*, p. 39.
8. Ibid., 45.

Introduction

1. "As I See It," *Rural Electrification Magazine*, October 1968, p. 2.
2. Remarks by President Barack Obama on the National Wireless Initiative in Marquette, Michigan, February 10, 2011, The White House, Office of the Press Secretary.
3. A Brief History of the Rural Electric and Telephone Programs, USDA Rural Electrification Administration.
4. Duane Noland, interview with author.
5. Remarks by President Barack Obama, February 10, 2011.
6. David Kennedy speech, November 1, 2012, Portland, Oregon.
7. Brown, *Electricity for Rural America*, p. 53.
8. Ibid., 61.
9. Remarks by President Barack Obama, February 10, 2011.

10. Clyde T. Ellis, *A Giant Step* (New York: Random House, 1966), p. 74.
11. Glenn English speech to NRECA Region VII–IX, October 2012.
12. Raymond Kuhl, "Mr. Rural Electrification," *Rural Electrification Magazine,* July 2011.
13. Ted Morgan, *FDR* (New York: Simon & Schuster, 1985), pp. 494–95.
14. Richard A. Pence, *The Next Greatest Thing* (Washington, D.C.: National Rural Electric Cooperative Association, 1984), p. 127.
15. Jimmy Carter, *Turning Point* (New York: Random House, Inc., 1992), p. 6.
16. David McCullough, *Truman* (New York: Simon & Schuster, 1992), p. 230.
17. Morgan, *FDR*, p. 494.

Chapter One: The Battle of Barnesville

1. Smith, *FDR*, p. 413.
2. Susan Dunn, *Roosevelt's Purge,* (Cambridge, Massachusetts: The Belknap Press of Harvard University Press: 2010), Kindle Edition, p. 1622.
3. Ibid., 1619.
4. *Rural Electrification News*, 1938.
5. Dunn, *Roosevelt's Purge*, p. 1708.
6. Ibid.
7. Ibid., 1627.
8. Ibid., 1628.
9. Smith, *FDR*, p. 478.
10. Address of President Franklin Delano Roosevelt, Barnesville, Georgia, Thursday, August 11, 1938, http://georgiainfo.galileo.usg.edu/FDRspeeches/FDRspeech38-6.htm
11. Dunn, *Roosevelt's Purge*, p. 1634.
12. Address of President Roosevelt, Barnesville, Georgia, August 11, 1938.
13. Address of President Roosevelt, Barnesville, Georgia, August 11, 1938.
14. Address of President Roosevelt, Barnesville, Georgia, August 11, 1938.
15. Dunn, *Roosevelt's Purge*, p.1733.
16. Address of President Roosevelt, Barnesville, Georgia, August 11, 1938.
17. "Roosevelt Asks Defeat of George and Talmadge as Foes of Liberalism," *The New York Times*, August 12, 1938, p. 4.
18. Ibid.
19. *Rural Electrification News,* 1938.
20. Paul Wood, interview with author.
21. Kenneth Davis, *FDR: Into the Storm* (New York: Random House, Inc., 1993), p. 280.
22. Dunn, *Roosevelt's Purge*, p. 1750.

23. Davis, *FDR: Into the Storm*, p. 280.

24. Dunn, *Roosevelt's Purge*, p. 1752.

25. Phillip Ramati, "Barnesville Remembers 1938 FDR Visit," OnLineAthens, *Athens Banner Herald*, October 11, 2009, http://onlineathens.com/stories/101109/new_503452879.shtml

26. Raleigh Henry, Interview with Author, January 14, 2013.

27. Smith, *FDR*, p. 414.

28. Ibid., 415.

29. Ibid.

30. Dunn, *Roosevelt's Purge*, p. 78.

31. Raleigh Henry, interview with author.

32. Dunn, *Roosevelt's Purge*, p. 217.

33. James Alonzo Bishop, *FDR's Last Year* (New York: William Morrow and Company, 1974), p. 522.

34. Ibid.

35. Ibid., 523.

36. Ibid., 525.

37. Ibid.

38. *Rural Electrification News*, 1944.

39. Ellis, *A Giant Step*, p. 63.

40. Ibid.

41. Brown, *Electricity for Rural America*, p. 77.

42. Robert A. Caro, *The Years of Lyndon Johnson* (New York: Alfred A. Knopf, 1983), p. 576.

43. Bishop, *FDR's Last Year*, p. 526.

44. Jean Edward Smith, *Lucius D. Clay* (New York: Henry Holt and Company, 1990), p. 216.

45. Brown, *Electricity for Rural America*, pp. 36–39.

46. Michael Callahan, interview with author.

47. Smith, *Lucius D. Clay*, p. 216.

48. Bishop, *FDR's Last Year*, p. 526.

49. "Spotlight on the REA 75th Anniversary," www.georgiaemc.com (see page 7).

50. Smith, *FDR,* p. 357.

51. Smith, *Lucius D. Clay,* p. 216.

52. McCullough, *Truman*, p. 341.

53. David M. Kennedy, *Freedom From Fear,* (New York: Oxford University Press, 1999), p. 790.

54. McCullough, *Truman*, p. 379.

55. Gene Tollefson, *BPA & the Struggle for Power at Cost* (Portland: Bonneville Power Administration, 1987), p. 234.

56. Pence, *The Next Greatest Thing*, p. 177.
57. Ibid., 179.
58. Frank K. Gallant, "Flashbacks," *Rural Electrification Magazine,* August 2003, p. 7.

Chapter Two: How About That Farm Vote?

1. "1948 Regional Meetings Get Underway," *Rural Electrification Magazine,* October 1948, p. 16.
2. McCullough, *Truman*, p. 654
3. "1948 Regional Meetings Get Underway," p. 16.
4. McCullough, *Truman*, p. 657.
5. "1948 Regional Meetings Get Underway," p. 16.
6. President Harry S. Truman, "Remarks of the President," Rural Electrification Cooperative Association Regional Meeting (Washington, D.C.), September 16, 1948.
7. Ted Sorensen, *Counselor* (New York: HarperCollins, 2008), p. 44.
8. Truman, "Remarks of the President."
9. Pence, *The Next Greatest Thing*, p. 179.
10. Truman, "Remarks of the President."
11. McCullough, *Truman*, p. 656.
12. Ibid.
13. Ibid., 657
14. Ibid.
15. Zachary Karabell, *The Last Campaign: How Harry Truman Won The 1948 Election* (New York: Vintage Books, 2001), p. 19.
16. McCullough, *Truman*, p. 657.
17. President Harry S. Truman, "Rear Platform and Other Informal Remarks in Illinois, Iowa and Missouri" (Oxford, Iowa), September 18, 1948, The American Presidency Project.
18. Marquis W. Childs, *Yesterday Today and Tomorrow* (Washington, D.C.: National Rural Electric Cooperative Association, 1980), p. 128.
19. McCullough, *Truman*, p. 668.
20. *Congressional Quarterly*, "Congress and the Nation: A Review of Government and Politics in the Postwar Years 1946–1964" (Washington D.C., *Congressional Quarterly*, 1964), p. 752.
21. McCullough, *Truman*, p. 677.
22. Ibid., 676.
23. President Harry S. Truman, "Address at Bonham, Texas" (Bonham, Texas), September 27, 1948.

24. President Harry S. Truman, "Rear Platform and Other Informal Remarks in Oklahoma and Missouri" (Shawnee and Seminole, Oklahoma), September 29, 1948.
25. McCullough, *Truman*, p. 663.
26. Ibid., 663–64.
27. M.W. Halloran, "State Plans 'Biggest Dewey Rally,'" *Minneapolis Star*, October 15, 1948.
28. President Harry S. Truman, "Rear Platform Remarks in Minnesota and Wisconsin" (Mankato, Minnesota), October 14, 1948, The American Presidency Project.
29. William Mylander, "Truman Raps Opponents on Co-op Policy," *Minneapolis Star*, October 15, 1948.
30. McCullough, *Truman*, p. 669.
31. Ibid., 703.
32. Karabell, *The Last Campaign*, p. 253.
33. McCullough, *Truman*, p. 707.
34. David Pietrusza, *1948* (New York: Union Square Press, 2011), p. 393
35. Karabell, *The Last Campaign*, p. 254.
36. McCullough, *Truman*, p. 712.
37. Pietrusza, *1948*, p. 405.
38. Karabell, *The Last Campaign*, p. 258.
39. Ibid., 257.
40. McCullough, *Truman*, p. 712.
41. Clyde Ellis telegraph to President Truman, November 1948, Truman Papers, Truman Library.
42. "Ellis Presents Rural Systems' Problems to President Personally," *Rural Electrification*, 1948.
43. Merle Miller, *Plain Speaking, An Oral Biography of Harry S. Truman* (New York: A Berkley Book, 1974), p. 272.
44. Jerry N. Hess, *Oral History Interview with Philip W. Voltz* (Glen Echo, Maryland), November 14, 1969.
45. Barry Hart, email to author, April 17, 2012.
46. Ellis, *A Giant Step*, p. 88.
47. McCullough, *Truman*, p. 922.
48. Ellis, *A Giant Step*, p. 101.
49. Ibid., 104.
50. Ibid., 101.
51. Ibid., 105.
52. Ibid., 112.

Chapter Three: D-Day for REA

1. Ellis, *A Giant Step*, p. 9.
2. The President's Appointments, Sunday, February 11, 1959, Dwight D. Eisenhower Presidential Library.
3. "The Rural Electric Week: Co-ops and Administration Take Off Gloves in Annual Meeting Power Fight," *The Rural Electric Minuteman 34* (February 13, 1959), p 1.
4. Robert A. Caro, *The Passage of Power* (New York: Alfred A. Knopf, 2012), p. 433.
5. Memo by H. C., December 31, 1958, Dwight D. Eisenhower Presidential Library.
6. Ezra Benson to Dwight D. Eisenhower, January 15, 1959, Dwight D. Eisenhower Presidential Library.
7. Ellis, *A Giant Step*, p. 16.
8. Stephen E. Ambrose, *Eisenhower: Soldier and President* (New York: Simon & Schuster, 1991), p. 473.
9. President's Appointments, February 11, 1959, Dwight D. Eisenhower Presidential Library.
10. Dwight D. Eisenhower, *A Mandate for Change 1953–1956* (New York: Doubleday & Company, Inc., 1963), p. 392.
11. Bud Wells, *Four Score for Dave Hamil* (Texas: Henington Publishing Company, 1988), p. 102.
12. Ellis, *A Giant Step*, p. 11.
13. Ibid., 15.
14. Ibid., 17.
15. Caro, *The Passage of Power*, p. 84.
16. Ellis, *A Giant Step*, p. 17.
17. Ibid.
18. Dwight D. Eisenhower, Remarks at the 7th Annual Meeting of the National Rural Electric Cooperative Association, (Washington, D.C.), February 11, 1959, The American Presidency Project.
19. Don Paarlberg to Jack Z. Anderson, January 29, 1959, Dwight D. Eisenhower Presidential Library.
20. Dwight D. Eisenhower, *Remarks*.
21. Ellis, *A Giant Step*, p. 17.
22. William M. Blair, "Eisenhower Seeks a Cut In Co-op Aid," *The New York Times,* February 12, 1959.
23. Ibid.
24. Presidential Appointments, February 11, 1959, Dwight D. Eisenhower Presidential Library.

25. Blair, "Eisenhower Seeks a Cut."

26. Clyde T. Ellis, "From Where I Sit," *Rural Electrification News,* March 1959, p. 5.

27. Dwight D. Eisenhower to Ezra Taft Benson, February 13, 1959, "In the Papers of Dwight David Eisenhower," Dwight D. Eisenhower Presidential Library.

28. Ellis, *A Giant Step,* p. 19.

29. Ibid.

30. *Ogden Standard Examiner,* April 28, 1959.

31. Ezra Taft Benson, *Cross Fire, The Eight Years With Eisenhower* (Garden City, New York: Doubleday & Company, Inc., 1962), p. 452.

32. Ellis, *A Giant Step,* p. 21.

33. Gerald R. Ford, *"Your Washington Review,"* May 20, 1959, Gerald R. Ford Congressional Papers at the Gerald R. Ford Presidential Library.

34. Benson, *Cross Fire, The Eight Years With Eisenhower,* p. 452.

35. "The Presidency: Man of the Year," *Time Magazine,* January 4, 1960.

36. Ellis, *A Giant Step.*

37. Eisenhower, *Mandate for Change,* pp. 393–94.

38. "Ike is Special Guest: Electric Cooperative Notes 25th Anniversary," *The Evening Sun,* August 5, 1965, p. 2.

39. Susan Eisenhower, Statement, NRECA Annual Meeting (Orlando, Florida), March 8, 2011.

40. Eisenhower, *Mandate for Change,* p. 394.

Chapter Four: The Poles and Wires of November

1. Arthur M. Schlesinger, Jr., *A Thousand Days* (Boston: Houghton Mifflin Company, 1965), p. 665.

2. "To the Brink, JFK and the Cuban Missile Crisis," exhibition created by the National Archives.

3. Ted Sorensen, *Counselor* (New York: Harper Collins, 2008), p. 1.

4. Laurence Chang and Peter Kornbluh, *The Cuban Missile Crisis, 1962* (New York: The New Press, 1992), p. 249.

5. David G. Coleman, *The Fourteenth Day* (New York: W. W. Norton & Company, 2012), p. 36.

6. The Presidents Engagements, November 1, 1962, John F. Kennedy Presidential Library.

7. Robert Dallek, *An Unfinished Life: John F. Kennedy 1917–1963* (New York: Little Brown & Company, 2003), p. 20.

8. Ellis, *A Giant Step,* p. 145.
9. Remarks of Senator John F. Kennedy at Antigo, Wisconsin, February 15, 1960, John F. Kennedy Presidential Library.
10. Glenn English, interview with author, January 2012.
11. Ellis, *A Giant Step,* p. 146–47.
12. Ibid., 156.
13. Theodore H. White, *The Making of the President 1960* (Montreal, Canada: Pocket Books of Canada, LTD, 1961), p. 333.
14. Ellis, *A Giant Step,* p. 161.
15. Ibid., 206.
16. James Giglio, *The Presidency of John F. Kennedy* (Kansas: University Press of Kansas, 1991), p. 232.
17. Schlesinger, *A Thousand Days,* p. 187.
18. Ibid., 204.
19. Ellis, *A Giant Step,* p. 199.
20. Ibid., 210.
21. Ibid., 206.
22. Remarks of President at the Signing of the Agency for International Development's Contract with the National Rural Electrification Cooperation Association, November 1, 1962, John F. Kennedy Presidential Library.
23. Chang and Kronbluh, *The Cuban Missile Crisis, 1962,* p. 384.
24. Address by President Kennedy on Cuba, November 2, 1962, "American History From Revolution to Reconstruction and Beyond."
25. Dallek, *An Unfinished Life: John F. Kennedy 1917–1963,* p. 571.
26. John Kennedy, "Remarks at the Dedication of the Oahe Dam, Pierre, South Dakota, August 17, 1962," The American Presidency Project.
27. Alex Radin, *Public Power—Private Life* (Washington, D.C.: American Public Power Association), p. 268.
28. Frank Gallant, "Exporting the Co-op Way," *Rural Electrification Magazine,* January 2006, p. 7.
29. Ellis, Letter to the President, March 30, 1965, LBJ Library.

Chapter Five: The Texas Hill Country and Vietnam

1. Brian VanDeMark, *Into the Quagmire* (New York: Oxford University Press, 1991), p. 177.
2. Remarks to the National Rural Electric Cooperative Association, July 14, 1965, The American Presidency Project.

3. Theodore H. White, *The Making of a President 1964* (New York: Atheneum Publishers, 1965), p. 419.

4. Robert Dallek, *Flawed Giant* (New York: Oxford University Press, 1998), p. 184.

5. Michael Beschloss, *Reaching for Glory* (New York: Touchstone, 2001), p. 378.

6. At War in Vietnam, *The New York Times*, July 14, 1965, p. 36.

7. Doris Kearns, *Lyndon Johnson and the American Dream* (New York: Harper & Row, Publishers, Inc., 1976), p. 293.

8. Remarks to the National Rural Electric Cooperative Association, July 14, 1965, The American Presidency Project.

9. Robert Komer, Oral History Interview 1, tape 1, LBJ Library.

10. Robert Dallek, *Lone Star Rising* (New York: Oxford University Press, 1991), p. 177.

11. Ibid., 176.

12. Ellis, Letter to the President, March 30, 1965, LBJ Library.

13. Kenneth Crawford, "Washington: Escalated Welfare," *Newsweek*, June 28, 1965, p. 28.

14. "Senate Approves $5 million for Vietnam Electric Co-ops," *Rural Electrification Magazine*, 1965.

15. Remarks to the National Rural Electric Cooperative Association, July 14, 1965, The American Presidency Project.

16. Daily Diary of LBJ, July 14, 1965, LBJ Library.

17. VanDeMark, *Into the Quagmire*, p. 177.

18. Dallek, *Flawed Giant*, p. 273.

19. Ellis, *A Giant Step*, p. 218.

20. Merle Miller, *Lyndon: An Oral Biography* (New York: Ballantine Books, 1981), p. 466.

21. Robert Komer, Oral History Interview 1, tape 1, LBJ Library.

22. Beschloss, *Reaching for Glory*, pp. 345–46.

23. Recording of telephone conversation between Lyndon B. Johnson and Senator Richard Russell, June 2, 1966, Recordings and Transcripts of Conversations and Meetings, LBJ Library.

24. Vaughn Davis Bornet, *The Presidency of Lyndon Johnson* (Lawrence, Kansas: University Press of Kansas, 1983), p. 250.

25. Roy Reed, "President Urges Firmness on War," *The New York Times*, February 28, 1968.

26. Remarks at the National Rural Electric Cooperative Association Convention in Dallas, February 27, 1968, The American Presidency Project.

27. Roy Reed, "President Urges Firmness on War," *The New York Times,* February 28, 1968.

28. David Wise, "The Twilight of a President," *The New York Times Magazine,* November 3, 1968, p. 27.

29. Glenn English, interview with author.

30. Mike Williams, email to author, January 30, 2012.

31. Robert Dallek, *Lone Star Rising: Lyndon Johnson and His Times, 1908–1960* (New York: Oxford University Press, 1991), p. 183.

32. Wallace Tillman, interview with author, November 2, 2012.

33. Nixon Films Statement for Rural Electrics, *Rural Electrification Magazine,* October, 1968, p. 31.

34. Frank K. Gallant, "Flashbacks: REA's Black Friday," *Rural Electrification Magazine,* February 2007, p. 7.

Chapter Six: The Electric Co-op Tapes

1. "Watergate Conviction," *The New York Times,* February 1, 1973.

2. Richard Nixon, *RN, The Memoirs of Richard Nixon* (New York: Grosset & Dunlap, 1990), p. 762.

3. Ibid., 761.

4. Clifton Daniel, "Nixon to 1976 Candidates: Don't Be Eager Too Soon," *The New York Times,* February 1, 1973, p. 20.

5. The President's News Conference, January 31, 1973, The American Presidency Project.

6. Sarah McClendon, *Mr. President, Mr. President: My Fifty Years Covering the White House* (Santa Monica, California: General Publishing Group, 1996), p. 133.

7. The President's News Conference, January 31, 1973, The American Presidency Project.

8. Nixon Presidential Materials Staff, Tape Subject Log, Conversation 43-8, January 31, 1973, Nixon Presidential Library and Museum.

9. Nixon Presidential Materials Staff, Tape Subject Log, Conversation 43-10, January 31, 1973, Nixon Presidential Library and Museum.

10. *Congressional Quarterly Almanac,* 1973, p. 317.

11. Nixon Presidential Materials Staff, Tape Subject Log, Conversation 111-4 and 113-1, January 24, 1973, Nixon Presidential Library and Museum.

12. Nixon Presidential Materials Staff, Tape Subject Log, Conversation 113-2, January 26, 1973, Nixon Presidential Library and Museum.

13. Angus Hastings, interview with author.

14. Howard Crinklaw, interview with author, November 29, 2012.

15. William M. Blair, "Critics Rebuffed on Farm Slashes," *The New York Times*, January 5, 1973, p. 5.

16. *Congressional Quarterly Almanac*, 1973, p. 317.

17. Cancer on the Presidency, March 31, 1973, Presidential Recordings Program, Miller Center, http://whitehousetapes.net/transcript/nixon/cancer-presidency.

18. Stanley I. Kutler, *Abuse of Power: The New Nixon Tapes* (New York: The Free Press, 1997), p. 474.

19. Statement on Signing a Bill To Improve the Rural Electrification and Telephone Program, May 11, 1973, The American Presidency Project.

20. *Rural Electrification Newsletter*, May 18, 1973.

21. "Ford's Rural Electrification Record," *Rural Electric Newsletter*, August 9, 1974, p. 4.

Chapter Seven: One Day in the Valley

1. Gerald R. Ford, *A Time to Heal: The Autobiography of Gerald R. Ford* (New York: Harper & Row, 1979), p. 387.

2. Ibid., 384.

3. Larry Daughtrey and Frank Sullivan, "Ford Wooing Crossovers," *The Tennessean*, May 16, 1976, p. 1.

4. Edmund Morris, *Dutch: A Memoir of Ronald Reagan* (New York: Random House, Inc., 1999), p. 313.

5. Jules Witcover, *Marathon: The Pursuit of the Presidency* (New York: The Viking Press, 1977), p. 428.

6. David Callis, interview with author.

7. Gerald R. Ford Library.

8. Ford, *A Time to Heal: The Autobiography of Gerald R. Ford*, pp. 387–88.

9. Roland Evans and Robert Novak, "Reagan's TVA Statement Careful Miscalculation," *The Tennessean*, May 28, 1976.

10. Witcover, *Marathon: The Pursuit of the Presidency*, p. 428.

11. Raymond Kuhl, interview with author.

12. Gerald R. Ford, *Your Washington Review*, May 13, 1959, Gerald R. Ford Congressional Papers at the Gerald R. Ford Presidential Library.

13. "Ford Names Longshore for TVA Post," *Rural Electric Newsletter*, June 18, 1976, pp. 1–2.

14. Bernard Gwertzman, "Ford Says Lebanon Policy Is Undeterred by Killings," *The New York Times*, June 17, 1976, p. 16.

15. The Daily Diary of President Gerald R. Ford, June 16, 1976, Gerald R. Ford Presidential Library.
16. Gwertzman, "Ford Says Lebanon Policy Is Undeterred by Killings."
17. Memo from Matthew C. Freedman to Terrence O'Donnell, Rural Electric Cooperative Association Meeting with the President, June 16, 1976, Gerald R. Ford Presidential Library.
18. Gerald R. Ford statement, June 16, 1976, Gerald R. Ford Presidential Library.
19. Presidential Greeting to Students Representing the National Rural Electric Cooperative Association, June 16, 1976, Gerald R. Ford Presidential Library.
20. Matt Rhoades, interview with author.
21. Ford, *A Time to Heal: The Autobiography of Gerald R. Ford*, p. 390.
22. Wally Rustad, interview with author.
23. Glenn English, interview with author.
24. "Butz to Committee: The Job Is Done," *Rural Electric Newsletter*, February 20, 1976, p. 1.
25. Rich Larochelle, interview with author.
26. Ford, *A Time to Heal: The Autobiography of Gerald R. Ford*, p. 340.
27. John Robert Greene, *The Presidency of Gerald R. Ford* (Lawrence, Kansas: University Press of Kansas, 1995), p. 193.

Chapter Eight: The Elephant in the East Room

1. The Daily Diary of President Jimmy Carter, December 1, 1978, Jimmy Carter Presidential Library.
2. Jimmy Carter, *The White House Diary* (New York: Farrar, Straus and Giroux, 2010), p. 263.
3. Jimmy Carter, *"Federal Initiatives in Rural Areas,"* Remarks at a White House Briefing, December 1, 1978, Jimmy Carter Presidential Library.
4. Daily Diary of President Jimmy Carter, December 1, 1978.
5. Peter G. Bourne, *Jimmy Carter* (New York: A Lisa Drew Book/Scribner, 1997), p. 426.
6. Jimmy Carter, *Keeping Faith* (Toronto, Canada: Bantam Books, 1982), p. 79.
7. Memorandum for the President from Jack Watson and Anne Wexler, *Meeting With Rural Leaders to Discuss Administration Rural Initiatives and Rural Electrification*, December 1, 1978, Jimmy Carter Presidential Library.

8. Memorandum for the President, December 1, 1978.

9. Ibid.

10. Don Smith, interview with author.

11. "OMB Scheme Revealed," *Rural Electric Newsletter*, September 9, 1977.

12. Memorandum for the President from Jim McIntyre, *Study of REA Electric Loan Program*, November 30, 1978, Jimmy Carter Presidential Library.

13. Jimmy Carter, Remarks: Federal Initiatives in Rural Areas Remarks at a White House Briefing, December 1, 1978, The American Presidency Project.

14. Jimmy Carter, *Turning Point*, (New York: Times Books, 1992), p. 6.

15. Wally Rustad, interview with author.

16. Jimmy Carter, Remarks; Federal Initiatives in Rural Areas Remarks at a White House Briefing.

17. Carter, *White House Diary*, p. 310.

18. Carter, *Keeping Faith*, p. 78.

19. "Torpedo the Dams?" *Rural Electric Newsletter*, June 2, 1977.

20. Jimmy Carter, Remarks: Federal Initiatives in Rural Areas Remarks at a White House Briefing.

21. Bob Bergland, interview with author.

22. Jimmy Carter, Remarks: Federal Initiatives in Rural Areas Remarks at a White House Briefing.

23. Don Smith, interview with author.

24. Memorandum for the President from Jim McIntyre, *Study of REA Electric Loan Program*, November 30, 1978, Jimmy Carter Presidential Library.

25. "President Warns of Tight Budget," Rural Electrification, February 1979, p. 22.

26. Carter, *Keeping Faith*, p. 565

27. Remarks of Jimmy Carter, Lakeland, Florida, Rally, October 31, 1980, The American Presidency Project.

28. Remarks of Jimmy Carter, Greeting Members of the Association's Youth Tour, National Rural Electric Cooperative Association, June 14, 1978, The American Presidency Project.

29. Frank Stork, interview with author.

30. Frank K. Gallant, "Battling to Save REA," *Rural Electrification Magazine*, January 2012, p. 7.

31. J.C. Brown, *Rural Electric Sourcebook* (NRECA, Washington D.C., 1990), p. 3.

Chapter Nine: Below the Radar

1. David A. Stockman, *Triumph of Politics* (New York: Avon Books, 1986), p. 93.
2. Ibid., 96.
3. Ibid., 97.
4. Ibid.
5. Ibid., 161.
6. Ibid., 165.
7. Ibid., 99.
8. Glenn English, interview with author.
9. "Anti-REA Plan Beyond Ignorance," *Rural Electric Newsletter,* March 27, 1991, p. 2.
10. *Rural Electric Newsletter,* 1981.
11. Stockman, *Triumph of Politics*, p. 165.
12. Reagan Address to AFL-CIO, C-Span Video Library, March 30, 1981.
13. Edmund Morris, *Dutch: A Memoir of Ronald Reagan* (New York: Random House, Inc., 1999), p. 424.
14. Nomination of Harold V. Hunter to be Administrator of the Rural Electrification Administration, April 9, 1981, The American Presidency Project.
15. *Rural Electric Newsletter,* April 17, 1981.
16. *Rural Electric Newsletter*, May 18, 1981.
17. Stockman, *Triumph of Politics*, p. 165.
18. *Congressional Quarterly Almanac*, 1982, p. 257.
19. Bob Bergland, interview with author.
20. Wally Rustad, interview with author.
21. Wallace Tillman, interview with author.
22. "Mondale Sweeps Poll," *Rural Electric Newsletter*, October 26, 1984.
23. Rich Larochelle, interview with author.
24. "Mondale Tells Regional Meeting He Will Keep Rural Electric Promises," *Rural Electric Newsletter,* October 5, 1984.
25. *Rural Electric Newsletter,* October 1984.
26. Mike Ganley, interview with author.
27. David Goeller, "Administration Seeks to Rein In Agency That Electrified Rural America," *Associated Press*, July 26, 1987.
28. Stockman, *Triumph of Politics*, p. 166.
29. Glenn English, interview with author.
30. *Power of the River* (United States of America: Government Printing Office, 2012), p. 125.

31. "Bergland Assails Power Scheme," *Rural Electric Newsletter*, January 3, 1986.

32. Bob Bergland, interview with author.

33. Lawrence Kudlow Speech at CFC Forum, New York City, July 2012.

34. "Hill Enacts Cable TV Law Over Veto," *Congressional Quarterly Almanac*, 1992, p. 171.

35. *Rural Electric Newsletter*, September 25, 1992.

Chapter Ten: The Veto Override

1. George Bush, *All the Best* (New York: Lisa Drew Book/Scribner, 1999), p. 567.

2. "Hill Enacts Cable TV Law Over Veto," *Congressional Quarterly Almanac*, 1992, p. 171.

3. "United States: Cable Television," The Museum of Broadcast Communications, http://www.museum.tv/eotvsection. php?entrycode=unitedstatessc

4. Jeff Almen, "Open Land Opened Skies, NRTC: The Birth and Growth of a Great Idea," 2003, p. 12.

5. Bob Phillips, interview with author.

6. Jeff Almen, "Open Land Opened Skies, NRTC: The Birth and Growth of a Great Idea, 2003, p. 105.

7. *Congressional Quarterly Almanac*, p. 179.

8. Carolyn Herr Watts, interview with author.

9. "Rural TV Bill Goes to Bush with Veto-Proof Hill Backing," *Rural Electric Newsletter*, September 25, 1992.

10. Rich Larochelle, interview with author.

11. David Mervin, *George Bush and the Guardianship Presidency* (New York: St. Martin's Press, 1996), p. 114.

12. Ibid., 116.

13. Edmund L. Andrews, "Bush Rejects Bill That Would Limit Rates on Cable TV," *The New York Times*, October 4, 1992.

14. *The New York Times*, October 4, 1992.

15. *Congressional Quarterly Almanac*, p. 183.

16. *The New York Times*, October 4, 1992.

17. *Congressional Record*, October 5, 1992.

18. *Congressional Record*, October 5, 1992.

19. *Congressional Record*, October 5, 1992.

20. *Congressional Quarterly Almanac*, p. 183.

21. "Cable Bill Surmounts Bush Veto," *Rural Electric Newsletter,* October 9, 1992, p. 3.
22. Adam Clymer, "Congress Rebuffs Bush in Override of Cable TV Veto, *The New York Times,* October 6, 1992.
23. Jeff Almen, "Open Land Opened Skies, NRTC: The Birth and Growth of a Great Idea," 2003, p. 116.
24. Bob Bergland, interview with author.
25. David Kusnet, email to author, June 19, 2012.
26. "Bush, Clinton Offer REA Views," *Rural Electric Newsletter,* October 9, 1992.
27. John Vanvig, "The Rural Electric Vote: Where Bush and Clinton stand on Co-op issues," *Rural Electrification,* November 1992, p. 20.

Chapter Eleven: Sacred Cows in the Margins

1. Bill Gorman, "State of the Union Address TV Ratings," *TV By the Numbers,* February 26, 2009, http://www.tvbythenumbers.zapit.com/2009/02/26/state-of-the-union-address-tv-ratings/13569
2. 1993 State of the Union Address, *The Washington Post,* February 17, 1993, http://www.washingtonpost.com/wp-srv/politics/special/states/docs/sou93.htm
3. Mary McGrory, "Preside and Conquer," *The Washington Post,* February 21, 1993, p. C–1.
4. 1993 State of the Union Address.
5. Ibid.
6. Glenn English, interview with author.
7. Wally Rustad, inteview with author.
8. Frank Gallant, "Flashbacks: Fighting for Fair Treatment," *Rural Electrification,* August 2011, p. 7.
9. Stephan Petry, interview with author.
10. George Stephanopoulos, *All Too Human* (New York: Back Bay Books, 2000), pp. 134–35.
11. William Jefferson Clinton, *My Life* (New York: Alfred N. Knopf, 2004), p. 493.
12. Gallant, "Flashbacks: Fighting for Fair Treatment."
13. Bob Woodward, *The Agenda* (New York, Simon & Schuster, 1994), p. 121.
14. Administration History, National Economic Council, 1993, William Jefferson Clinton Presidential Library.

15. Woodward, *The Agenda*, p. 131.

16. David Kusnet, email to author, June 19, 2012.

17. Glenn English, interview with author.

18. Kevin Merida, "The Lights are Flickering at REA," *The Washington Post,* May 2, 1993, p. 1.

19. Remarks on the Economic Program in St. Louis, Missouri, February 18, 1993, Administration of William J. Clinton, 1993, p. 124.

20. Remarks to the Cleveland City Club, May 10, 1993, The American Presidency Project.

21. Gallant, "Flashbacks: Fighting for Fair Treatment."

22. Full Text of REA Budget Proposals, U.S. Government Printing Office, March 16, 1993.

23. Merida, "The Lights are Flickering at REA."

24. Rich Larochelle, interview with author.

25. Glenn English, interview with author.

26. William J. Clinton Statement on Signing the Rural Electrification Loan Restructuring Act of 1993, November 1, 1993, The American Presidency Project.

27. Kevin Merida, "Revamped REA Will Cost Less, Play Broader Role," *The Washington Post,* November 21, 1993.

28. Gallant, "Flashbacks: Fighting for Fair Treatment."

29. *Congressional Quarterly Almanac,* 1993, p. 228.

30. Remarks at a Town Meeting in Billings, Montana, June 1, 1995, Administration of William J. Clinton, 1995.

31. Bob Bergland, interview with author.

32. Mark Glaess, interview with author.

33. Glenn English, interview with author.

34. Administration Histories, Department of Energy, Weekly Activity Report, 1995, William J. Clinton Presidential Library.

35. "The Potential Transfer of the Power Marketing Administrations out of Federal Ownership," Oversight Hearing Before the Subcommittee on Water and Power Resources of the Committee on Resources, House of Representatives, 104th Congress, May 19, 1995.

36. Remarks at a Town Meeting in Billings, Montana, June 1, 1995, Administration of William J. Clinton, 1995.

37. "On the Record," *Rural Electrification Magazine,* November 1996.

38. Wally Rustad, interview with author.

39. "On the Record," *Rural Electrification Magazine,* November 1996.

40. Rich Glick, interview with author.

Chapter Twelve: Punching Above Their Weight

1. Robert Draper, *Dead Certain* (New York: Free Press, 2007), p. 305.
2. George W. Bush, *Decision Points* (New York: Crown Publishers, 2010), p. 313.
3. White House Press Release, "President Signs Energy Policy Act," August 8, 2005, George W Bush White House Archives.
4. Keven Groenewold, interview with author.
5. Keven Groenewold, interview with author.
6. Mike Williams, interview with author.
7. Dick Cheney, *In My Time (New York: Simon & Schuster, Inc, 2011),* pp. 315–16.
8. Ibid., 316.
9. Glenn English, "Politics and Policy Affecting NRECA Members, Commentary," *Rural Electrification Magazine,* July 2001, p. 10.
10. "WP Politics: Thomas Kuhn," *The Washington Post,* www.washington post.com/politics/thomas-kuhn/glQAc9ZTAP_topic.html
11. "Energy & Environment: Energy Overhaul Includes Many Bush Priorities—But Not ANWR," *Congressional Quarterly Almanac,* 2005.
12. Bush, *Decision Points*, p. 127.
13. Rich Bauer, interview with author.
14. Bush, *Decision Points*, p.131.
15. Rich Bauer, interview with author.
16. "The 9/11 Commission Report" (New York: W.W. Norton & Company), p. 14.
17. Bush, *Decision Points*, p. 132.
18. Bauer, interview with author.
19. White House Press Release, "President Signs Energy Policy Act," August 8, 2005, George W. Bush White House Archives.
20. Peter Nye, "Grassroots," *Rural Electrification Magazine,* September 2005, p. 25.
21. Peter Nye, "Co-ops and the Energy Policy Act," *Rural Electrification Magazine,* January 2006, pp. 24–28.
22. Keven Groenewold, interview with author.
23. George Stuteville, "NRECA Legislative Conference: 'Democracy in Action,'" *Electric Co-op Today,* May 9, 2003, p. 4.
24. Chuck Penry, interview with author.
25. Lisa Epifani, interview with author.
26. Frank Stork, "The Great Builder," *Rural Missouri,* August 2003, p. 5.
27. Don Smith, interview with author.

28. Stork, "The Great Builder," p. 5.
29. White House Press Release, "President Signs Energy Policy Act," August 8, 2005, George W. Bush White House Archives.
30. Jay Morrison, interview with author.
31. White House Press Release, "President Signs Energy Policy Act," August 8, 2005, George W. Bush White House Archives.
32. Bush, *Decision Points*, p. 347.
33. Glenn English, interview with author.
34. Glenn English, interview with author.
35. Rick Haile, interview with author.
36. Bush, *Decision Points*, p. 312.

Afterword: Dusting Off the Playbook

1. Jon Cohen, "Mitt Romney reaches out to voters but often lacks the common touch," *The Washington Post*, October 21, 2011.

INDEX

NOTE: Page numbers followed by the italicized letter *p*
indicate material found in photos.

ACKNOWLEDGMENTS

THIS BOOK WOULD NOT HAVE BEEN POSSIBLE WITHOUT THE generosity of many people. First, the insights and friendship of Bob Bergland and Glenn English were invaluable in making this narrative possible. Along with Clyde Ellis and Bob Partridge, they are the true giants of the electric co-op program.

Then there are the other political warriors, in no particular order, who fought these battles and helped bring these stories alive: Mattie Olson, Don Smith, Wally Tillman, Frank Stork, Rich Larochelle, Carolyn Herr Watts, Martin Lowery, Bob Phillips, Sheldon Peterson, Carmie Henry, Mike Ganley, Dena Stoner, Chuck Penry, Kirk Johnson, Jim Jura, Ron Greenhalgh, Frank Gallant, Ray Kuhl, Mike Guidry, and many others. If I missed you—you know who you are. Former NRECA greats Wally Rustad and Steve Petry hired me into the electric co-op family, and for that, I am eternally grateful. It changed my life.

I want to give a nod to my brother and sisters at NRECA and the Rural Electric Statewide Managers Association who provided help for this book. May we write more chapters in this amazing co-op history.

Special thanks to my editor, Peter Nyc. Not only did he sharpen the text, he made me believe I may have a story to tell. Perry Stambaugh, the outstanding editor of *Rural Electrification Magazine*, was a tremendous help. Shannon Bodie designed a brilliant cover and kept the project on track. Jann Armstrong, Palma Odano, Magen Howard, and Bob Smith helped turn a mess of pages into an actual book.

Thanks to Laura Schepis and her team for letting me raid the NRECA library, and to Bob Speckman for letting me into his splendid archive. Our presidential libraries contain a treasure trove of materials, and thanks to those who helped me when I visited or emailed. Every American should visit them. Mark Glaess, Adam Schwartz, Crystal Ball, and Lisa Logie looked at early drafts of *Power Plays*, and all made important suggestions.

Thanks also to the Board of the Oregon Rural Electric Cooperative Association. They allowed me to have a day job so I could write this book on the weekends. ORECA is a great organization with a storied history worthy of a book of its own.

A special thanks to my wonderful mother, Ruth, for giving me a love of books and so much more. And, of course, a special thanks to my sister, Jeanine, and my brother-in-law, Doug, the world's coolest people. Along with the whole Rasmussen clan, they urged me to carry this project through to the end. My own adorable children, Malia and Jack, were incredibly patient and interested in this project. I hope someday they will write their own stories.

Finally, my deep appreciation and love for my wife, Nicole, who allowed me to write, read countless drafts, typed up footnotes, and never doubted the book would see the light of day, even when I did.

She is who I write for.

ABOUT THE AUTHOR

Tᴇᴅ Cᴀsᴇ ɪs ᴛʜᴇ ᴇxᴇᴄᴜᴛɪᴠᴇ ᴅɪʀᴇᴄᴛᴏʀ ᴏꜰ ᴛʜᴇ Oʀᴇɢᴏɴ Rural Electric Cooperative Association in Salem, Oregon. From 1997–2008, he served in the Government Relations Department of the National Rural Electric Cooperative Association in Arlington, Virginia. He has a M.A. in Fiction Writing from Johns Hopkins University. He lives in Wilsonville, Oregon, with his wife, Nicole, and two children, Malia and Jack.